FUNNY ANIMALS! COLLECTION

NATIONAL GEOGRAPHIC

WASHINGTON, D.C.

Inside This BOOK

DON'T MISS:
To the Rescue!

Book 1

PARROT GENIUS!

And More True Stories of Amazing Animal Talents

Moira Rose Donohue

Published by the National Geographic Society

Gary E. Knell, *President and Chief Executive Officer*
John M. Fahey, *Chairman of the Board*
Declan Moore, *Executive Vice President; President, Publishing and Travel*
Melina Gerosa Bellows, *Publisher and Chief Creative Officer, Books, Kids, and Family*

Prepared by the Book Division
Hector Sierra, *Senior Vice President and General Manager*
Nancy Laties Feresten, *Senior Vice President, Kids Publishing and Media*
Jennifer Emmett, *Vice President, Editorial Director, Kids Books*
Eva Absher-Schantz, *Design Director, Kids Publishing and Media*
Jay Sumner, *Director of Photography, Kids Publishing*
R. Gary Colbert, *Production Director*
Jennifer A. Thornton, *Director of Managing Editorial*

Staff for This Book
Shelby Alinsky, *Project Editor*
Amanda Larsen, *Art Director*
Kelley Miller, *Senior Photo Editor*
Ruth Ann Thompson, *Designer*
Marfé Ferguson Delano, *Editor*
Ariane Szu-Tu, *Editorial Assistant*
Callie Broaddus, *Design Production Assistant*
Grace Hill, *Associate Managing Editor*
Joan Gossett, *Production Editor*
Lewis R. Bassford, *Production Manager*
Susan Borke, *Legal and Business Affairs*

Production Services
Phillip L. Schlosser, *Senior Vice President*
Chris Brown, *Vice President, NG Book Manufacturing*
George Bounelis, *Senior Production Manager*
Nicole Elliott, *Director of Production*
Rachel Faulise, *Manager*
Robert L. Barr, *Manager*

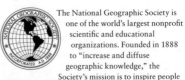

The National Geographic Society is one of the world's largest nonprofit scientific and educational organizations. Founded in 1888 to "increase and diffuse geographic knowledge," the Society's mission is to inspire people to care about the planet. It reaches more than 400 million people worldwide each month through its official journal, *National Geographic,* and other magazines; National Geographic Channel; television documentaries; music; radio; films; books; DVDs; maps; exhibitions; live events; school publishing programs; interactive media; and merchandise. National Geographic has funded more than 10,000 scientific research, conservation, and exploration projects and supports an education program promoting geographic literacy.

For more information, please visit nationalgeographic.com, call 1-800-NGS LINE (647-5463), or write to the following address:

National Geographic Society, 1145 17th Street N.W., Washington, D.C. 20036-4688 U.S.A.

Visit us online at nationalgeographic.com/books

For librarians and teachers: ngchildrensbooks.org

National Geographic supports K–12 educators with ELA Common Core Resources. Visit natgeoed.org/commoncore for more information.

More for kids from National Geographic: kids.nationalgeographic.com

For information about special discounts for bulk purchases, please contact National Geographic Books Special Sales: ngspecsales@ngs.org

For rights or permissions inquiries, please contact National Geographic Books Subsidiary Rights: ngbookrights@ngs.org

Trade paperback
ISBN: 978-1-4263-1770-5
Reinforced library edition
ISBN: 978-1-4263-1771-2

Printed in China
14/RRDS/1

Table of CONTENTS

Einstein is especially curious. That makes her easy to train.

EINSTEIN: PARROT GENIUS!

Einstein joined
the Knoxville Zoo
in Tennessee
when she was
five years old.

IT'S A ZOO HERE!

Imagine you're at the zoo. You hear a tiger growl. That's not surprising. Lots of zoos have tigers. But what if you're nowhere near the tiger exhibit? Next you hear a chimp screech. But there are no chimps around. And then a pirate says, *"Arrgh!"* Is it some kind of trick? Not if you're at the Knoxville (sounds like NOX-vil) Zoo in Knoxville, Tennessee, U.S.A.

It means you've just found Einstein, one of the most amazing parrots in the world!

Einstein joined the Knoxville Zoo more than 20 years ago. The zoo wanted to put together an animal show. It hired an animal talent scout. That's someone who looks for awesome animals that can learn to perform. When the talent scout heard about a very smart five-year-old parrot named Einstein, he knew he had to meet her.

Einstein is an African gray parrot. In the wild, African grays live in large groups called flocks. Some flocks have 100 birds. Living in such large groups makes them social, or friendly, with each other.

African gray parrots live in the rain

forests of Africa. But Einstein was not born in Africa. She was hatched in California. Einstein's owners could tell that she was extra smart. That's why they named her after the scientist Albert Einstein. He was so smart that people called him a genius!

The talent scout drove over to meet Einstein. *Would she be as brainy as her namesake?* He hoped so. The breeders introduced him to Einstein. Einstein turned her head this way and that. Then she said a few words to him. That's right—she spoke!

All African gray parrots can mimic sounds. But not all African grays choose to do so. The scout could see that Einstein was naturally chatty. She would be easy to train. He took her to the Knoxville Zoo to try her out for the show.

Parrot Primer

Let's talk parrots:

- There are over 350 types of parrots in the world.
- Parrots usually live in tropical areas. But one type (above), the kea (sounds like KEE-eh), lives in the snowy mountains of southern New Zealand.
- Most parrots are brightly colored. Macaws (sounds like muh-KAWS) are some of the most colorful.
- All parrots have curved beaks.
- Most parrots eat seeds and fruit. Some eat flowers and bugs.
- Parrots have four toes on each foot. Two toes point forward and two point backward.
- The biggest parrots are the macaw (left) and the large cockatoo.

The trainers at the Knoxville Zoo put Einstein in her new home. They knew that like some people, parrots can be afraid of new places. But Einstein wasn't an ordinary parrot. She was curious. She checked out the parrot cage. It was big enough to hold a couple of large dogs. She saw that it had several perches, or branches. It also had three bowls. One was for water. Another was for food—berries and seeds. The third bowl was empty. Soon Einstein would find out what it was for.

In no time, Einstein made herself at home. Zoo trainers put toys in her cage. They gave her shiny beads to play with. They gave her bells to ring. Sometimes they hid food inside tubes. She liked to figure out how to get the food out!

It didn't take the zoo long to decide that Einstein would be good in the show. But she had to be trained. Scientists say that African grays are as smart as five-year-old children. But they behave like two-year-olds. That meant Einstein had a lot to learn.

Teresa Collins became her first head trainer at the zoo. Teresa knew the first thing Einstein needed to learn was to trust her. So she dropped treats into the third bowl in Einstein's cage whenever she walked by. Sometimes she tossed a peanut into the treat bowl. That was the best. Einstein loved peanuts! Einstein soon learned that Teresa made good things happen.

After a while, Teresa tried something new. Instead of dropping a treat into the bowl, she pinched the food between her fingers. She held it out to Einstein. African gray parrots have strong beaks. Teresa wanted Einstein to take the food gently. Einstein had learned that Teresa was her friend. She knew better than to bite the hand that fed her.

One day, Teresa put her hand into Einstein's cage. She hoped Einstein would climb onto it. It would mean that Einstein trusted her. Trusting a human can take time, so it's a big step for a parrot. But not for Einstein. Einstein went to Teresa right away. She even let Teresa pet her chest.

Did You Know?

Sometimes African gray parrots will shrink the pupils in their eyes, bob their heads, stretch their necks, and throw up. It's a sign that they love you!

Now Einstein was ready to learn some new words. *How quickly would she learn?* Teresa wondered. We say that African gray parrots "talk." But actually, they mimic, or copy, sounds. They have a lot of muscles (sounds like MUH-sels) in their necks. They use them to change how the air goes through their throats. That makes different sounds. It's kind of like playing a flute.

African grays can make 2,000 different sounds. It's fun for them. But it also protects them. In the wild, some large birds, like hawks, owls, and eagles, feed on parrots. If one grabs an African gray, the bird makes a loud noise. Screech! The large bird lets go of the parrot. Imagine you are about to take a bite of pizza. Suddenly, it screams. You'd drop it pretty fast, too!

Teresa wanted Einstein to copy her. She would speak a word to Einstein. Sometimes Einstein said the word right away. Sometimes Teresa had to repeat it over and over. Teresa discovered that Einstein liked saying lots of words. But sometimes she refused to repeat a word. Parrots will only make sounds they like.

Einstein didn't copy just the sounds her trainers made. She copied *any* sound she liked. She loved the sound of water running. So she taught herself that sound. Once she heard an embarrassing sound. Oops. Someone passed gas. Einstein copied that sound too. Maybe she needs to learn, "Excuse me!"

Parrots can feed themselves with their feet. But this brainy bird can do a whole lot more!

Chapter 2

One day Teresa had a brainstorm. Einstein lived in a zoo with all kinds of animals. *Would the parrot enjoy making animal sounds?* Teresa wondered. So Teresa howled like a wolf. *"Aaooo!"*

"Aaooo!" Einstein howled back.

"Whoo, whoo, whoooo!" Teresa hooted like an owl.

"Whoo, whoo, whoooo!"

Einstein hooted back. Einstein loved to imitate animal sounds.

After a while, Teresa decided to teach Einstein to make these sounds "on cue." That means making a sound in response to a question. It was harder to teach— and to learn!

First, Teresa waited for Einstein to copy a sound, like "meow." She gave Einstein a treat. Then she asked a question. "What does a cat say?" When Einstein said "meow" again, she got another treat. This time she got a big treat—a peanut! Teresa did this over and over. Soon Einstein said "meow" whenever Teresa asked her what a cat said.

One time Einstein heard a funny sound and started repeating it. It sounded like

"*Arrgh.*" It made her trainer think of a pirate. Pirates often had colorful parrots on their shoulders. So her trainer said, "What do pirates say?"

"*Arrgh,*" said Einstein. Teresa and Einstein said it over and over. In just a couple of hours, Einstein had a new sound on cue!

Teresa and the other trainers picked out new sounds for Einstein to learn. When they agreed on one, they would all say it to her whenever they saw her. Before long, Einstein could make 200 sounds, including many animal noises! That's more than almost any other parrot, even other African grays.

Did You Know?

Crows are also very intelligent birds. They can make and use tools. One crow was filmed making a wire hook to get food!

Einstein stood out because she knew a lot of sounds. And she learned fast. But there are other parrots that can make a lot of sounds. What makes Einstein extra special is that she *remembers* sounds on cue. Most other parrots can only remember 13 or 14 sounds on cue at a time. But that's not how Einstein's brain works. She doesn't forget old cues when she learns new ones. Einstein knows 85 words on cue. She really is amazing!

Does Einstein understand what she's saying? Her trainers say that's a hard question to answer. Sometimes the parrot says something that isn't right. One time, her trainer said, "Make an evil laugh." Usually Einstein says, "*Nyah-ah-ah.*" But this time, Einstein said, "I love you."

But sometimes she says things that make a lot of sense, even if she isn't given a cue. One day a trainer was eating in front of her. "What are you doing?" Einstein asked. She cocked her head. She was looking for a treat. When the trainer didn't give her one, she said, "*Mmmmm,*" like we say when something tastes really good. No one taught her that! Soon she started doing it whenever a trainer was eating. She was training her trainer to give her a treat!

Once Einstein didn't get a treat when she said "*Mmmmm.*" To get her trainers' attention, she lay on her back in her cage. She stuck her feet in the air. She looked right at her trainers. "What are you doing, sweetheart?" she asked. Her trainers thought she was complaining because she wasn't getting a treat. They laughed really hard and gave her one.

Dr. Irene Pepperberg, a scientist, believes that parrots understand language. She wanted to prove her idea. She had a parrot, an African gray parrot named Alex. She trained him and studied him for 30 years. Alex learned over 150 words. And he showed signs of understanding language. So maybe when Einstein seems to understand, she really does!

Even though Einstein knew a lot of words, she had other things to learn before she would be ready for the zoo's show. Her trainers taught her to get in and out of her cage when she was told. And they gave her treats when she stayed on her perch. But she had one more important thing to learn.

Alex, Another Awesome Parrot

Scientists have taught apes to understand human language. Dr. Pepperberg tried to do the same thing with her parrot, Alex. She showed him different colored things. Then she asked him to pick out something blue. He did, over and over. She asked him how many items he saw. He would count up to six things. Sometimes Alex asked for something. If Dr. Pepperberg gave him the wrong item, he told her. She thought this showed that he could understand.

In the show, called *Animals in Action,* Einstein would help teach visitors about parrots in the wild. She would also show them how birds are trained. But she would have to talk into a microphone so the audience could hear her.

Some parrots get shy about talking into a microphone. They move away. They stop talking. Teresa wondered how Einstein would react to the microphone.

"Here, Einstein," Teresa said. "Let's practice." She held up the microphone. It was the first time Einstein had seen one. But the chatty parrot wasn't nervous at all. She leaned in. She said all her words on cue. She was ready for the show!

The day of her first show soon arrived. The audience filed into the outdoor theater and took their seats. Einstein looked at them. Teresa asked her a question. She held up the microphone. Einstein answered. She asked another question. Einstein answered that too. She remembered everything. She really was a parrot genius!

The audience couldn't believe it. They clapped and clapped. They told their friends about Einstein. Soon everyone in Knoxville was talking about the brilliant parrot.

Shy away from a microphone? Not Einstein. This bird's a superstar!

Chapter 3

SUPERSTAR!

The people at a local TV show heard about Einstein. They invited her to be on the show. Soon she was invited to be on other radio and TV shows.

Then Einstein got her big break. She was invited to an animal talent show! By then Einstein had a new trainer—Stephanie White. She and Stephanie were going to be on national TV. It was a great chance for people to see what Einstein could do. And Stephanie wasn't worried. She knew Einstein was a natural performer.

Stephanie and Einstein flew to California, U.S.A. They waited backstage at the TV studio. Other animals performed. Then the announcer introduced Einstein. Stephanie and Einstein took the stage. Stephanie stood in front of a sparkly blue curtain covered with stars. She wore a green shirt and pants with pockets. That's where she kept treats for Einstein.

Einstein stood on a perch. She looked out at the bright lights. And the cameras. And the big audience. She had seen that all before. But there was something more this time. Three judges sat in front of the stage. This was more than just a TV show. It was also a talent *contest*.

Stephanie smiled at the audience. Then she held the microphone up to Einstein. "Are you excited?" she asked the bird.

"*Whoooo!*" said Einstein. Then Stephanie asked the parrot her name. Einstein made a funny sound. "*Unnh, unnh, unnh.*" It didn't sound like "Einstein." Uh-oh.

Stephanie frowned. Was Einstein suddenly camera shy? How embarrassing if Einstein didn't want to perform! Then she figured it out. "She's just clearing her throat," she said. Stephanie tried again. She asked Einstein to say her name.

"Einstein," she said. Nice and loud. And then she said, "Hi, sweetheart." Stephanie knew then that everything would be all right.

Protect the Parrots!

Wild African gray parrots live in Africa. But they are popular pets in other countries. So people in Africa catch them. They ship them around the world. But they're not always careful. Sometimes they wipe out entire flocks. Sometimes they don't care for the birds that are shipped. The birds die. Some countries try to protect parrots. Now people need permission to bring them into the United States. If you want a parrot for a pet, consider buying one from a local breeder.

She asked Einstein to make some animal sounds. Einstein howled like a wolf. Then she growled like a tiger. She mimicked a chimp and a pig. Then Stephanie said, "How about a skunk?"

Einstein said, "Stinker."

Then Stephanie told Einstein to make sound effects. Einstein made the sound of water going down a drain. Then she made a spaceship noise. She did her evil laugh. *Nyah-ah-ah.* The judges laughed. So did the audience. Einstein bobbed a little dance with Stephanie. She fluffed up her feathers.

Then Stephanie said she had a problem. "What's the matter?" asked Einstein. Stephanie told Einstein she had lost her dog. Einstein whistled. "Come here!" she said.

At the end of the show, Stephanie asked, "Are you famous?"

Einstein put her beak right up to the microphone. "Superstar!" she whispered. One judge's mouth fell open.

But Einstein was right. She was a superstar! And she won the talent contest! Now she really was famous. More TV shows invited her to appear. She was on *Good Morning America,* the *Early Show,* and the *Late Show.* She was even on the *Tonight Show.* The host was impressed. He had had birds on his show before. But Einstein was the only bird that did what she was supposed to do!

In 2008 Stephanie left the zoo. She became a teacher. Einstein got a new head trainer. Her name was Nikki Edwards.

Nikki grew up on a farm near Knoxville. Her father owned a pet store. She's always lived around animals. When she was little, she used to sit outdoors and stretch her arms out. She waited for birds to land on them. When she got older, Nikki wanted to work with animals. So she joined the circus. She was even in a circus act.

After a while, Nikki came home. She started working at the Knoxville Zoo. Now Nikki travels with Einstein to her appearances. They've toured all around the country. When they fly, Einstein travels in a small cage that fits under the seat.

One time there was a problem with their plane. It sat on the runway for several hours. People got nervous. Then a strange beeping sound started. Now the people on the plane were really worried. But Nikki wasn't. She bent down. She looked under the seat. "Be quiet, Einstein," she whispered. It wasn't the right time to make a noise like that!

Einstein sometimes makes mistakes when she performs. She might say, "No," when she is supposed to say, "Yes." When that happens, her trainers try to change the conversation. Sometimes it works. Sometimes they just have to laugh.

Laughing is actually Einstein's favorite sound to mimic. She does her evil laugh. And she does a great Santa Claus laugh. "Ho-ho-ho," she says in a deep voice. Sometimes she makes laughing sounds for

Did You Know?

The most common species of bird in the world is ... the chicken! Chickens can make over 30 sounds to warn about different dangers.

fun. That gets the trainers laughing. And then Einstein laughs even more!

In 2014, Einstein turned 27 years old. Einstein is very busy. She is now the star of the zoo. She and Nikki perform three shows a day during the summer. During the school year, they visit schools. They also visit local community centers. At their shows, Einstein and Nikki teach people about wild African grays. They show people what African gray parrots can do. And they teach everyone about being good pet owners.

Someday you might visit the Knoxville Zoo. You might hear a certain animal sound when there's no sign of that animal. But now you'll know what it is. It's the sound of a superstar!

Will and Otis soar above the clouds. Otis is as happy as a dog with his head out a car window.

OTIS: WHEN PUGS FLY

Otis looked at Will with big puppy eyes like this pug. Will knew this was the dog for him.

PUG or PIG?

One hot summer day in 2001, Will da Silva left his home near Sacramento, California. He drove to a house a few miles away. He was a little nervous. He wasn't sure what he would find there. But he was also excited. He was hoping to meet someone he would fall in love with.

Will knocked and a woman came to the door. "I've come about

your ad," Will said.

"Come on in," said the woman.

When Will stepped through the door, eight pairs of big, brown eyes looked at him. They belonged to eight pug puppies. They all had wrinkled, "pushed-in" faces. They looked as if they had walked into a door without opening it first! Pugs sometimes come in black, but these were all tan colored, with black faces and ears. Will had come to buy one of the puppies from the woman and her husband. Their pug was the mother of this litter of puppies.

The eight little pugs cocked their heads up at Will. It seemed like they were trying to figure him out. Then one puppy ran up to him. Will tickled his belly. The puppy licked Will's nose. When Will put him down, the pup pawed at Will's leg. He ran around in circles in front of Will. He wagged his curly little tail.

Will tried to play with the other puppies, but the first one wouldn't let him. He nudged the others away. He climbed over Will's feet. *Don't play with the others,* he seemed to say. *Pick me!*

The other puppies ran and barked and wrestled with one another. But not that first puppy. He followed Will around. He wouldn't leave him alone.

Will sat down and looked into the puppy's big eyes. Will had wanted a pug ever since he was a kid and saw a movie called *The Adventures of Milo and Otis.*

What's in a Name?

It's easy to see why some people might confuse pugs and pigs. Their names sound similar. They both have curly tails. They both snort. Some pigs are kept as family pets. But pugs are dogs, of course. The first pug dogs probably came from China. We don't know for sure how they got their name. It may have come from the Latin word *pugnus,* which means "fist." The word "pug" is also an old nickname for a monkey. And some monkeys have "pushed-in" faces—just like pugs!

The movie is about two best friends—a cat named Milo and a pug named Otis. The friends get separated. But they never give up looking for each other. Something about that pug's loyalty made Will want a pug of his own. And this puppy seemed loyal to Will already. *This was the puppy for him,* Will decided. He already knew what to name him. Otis, of course!

"Come on, Otis. Let's go home," Will said. He paid for the puppy and put him into the cardboard box he had brought. Off they went. Poor Otis cried and whined the whole ride. He wanted to get out of the box and run around.

When they got home, Will carried the box into his house. Otis hopped right out. He ran here and there, like he was looking for something. Then he ran in circles. *What in the world?* It was like the puppy wanted something. *Aha! Maybe Otis is hungry,* Will thought. He gave him a bowl of puppy chow. Otis gobbled it up. Then the pup wanted dessert. He found it— Will's sandal! *Mmmmm.* It became his favorite toy.

After Otis finished eating, Will decided it was time to introduce the puppy to his other dog, Rocky. Rocky was big and strong. He was a Rottweiler (sounds like ROT-wy-ler). Rottweilers were bred to work as guard dogs or herding dogs. But they are also family pets, like Rocky. Rocky was black with tan on his face and paws. His coloring was the opposite of Otis's.

Will carried Otis over to Rocky.
Otis hung back. His curly tail uncurled.
The puppy seemed a little bit afraid.
After all, Rocky's head alone was bigger
than all of Otis!

Then Otis noticed the couch. It was
long way up for a little puppy. He backed
up, crouched down, and sprang! He made
it. Then he climbed even higher, all the
way to the top. "He found his spot on
the top of the couch cushion," Will said.
It would soon become his favorite spot to
sit or to nap.

Of course, Rocky jumped onto the
couch too. Otis's wrinkled face looked
nervous. But he didn't need to be worried.
Rocky sniffed Otis with his big nose.
Then he snuggled up right next to Otis.

In no time, Rocky became like a big brother to him. He played with Otis. He even licked Otis's ears to clean them out.

Otis loved Will's daughter, Nicole, from the start. Nicole liked to put on shows and dress up in costumes. One day she might be a princess. Another day, Nicole was a rock star. Sometimes she needed another actor for her plays. "Otis, you be the clown," she would say. Then she dressed him up too. Otis didn't mind. He sat there quietly, cocking his head and looking cute.

Otis adored Will and Rocky and Nicole. But more than anything, he loved food. Especially bacon. When he wanted a snack, he ran in circles. *Give me treats,* he seemed to say. He even stole Rocky's food when Rocky wasn't looking. But Rocky didn't do anything. He just let Otis have his food. Will called Otis an "eat-aholic."

Sometimes Otis ate strange things— things that weren't food at all. One day Nicole opened her crayon box and found that some colors were gone. "Dad! Crayons are missing again," she reported. They both knew what had happened. Otis had stolen them. But he couldn't help himself. To him they were "pug-a-licious." He couldn't hide his crime, either. After Otis ate crayons, his poop came out rainbow colored. Otis the pug loved to pig out!

Otis shows off the special harness created for him by parachute maker Pete Swan.

Chapter 2

High-Flying PUG

Otis always looked sad when Will left for work. And Will hated leaving the puppy at home. One day he had his hand on the doorknob and was about to leave when he thought, *I wonder if Otis would like to come with me.*

"Hey, Otis," he called. "Want to go to work with me?" The pug perked up. "OK, let's go then!"

Will said. Otis hopped into the car with him and off they went.

Will taught skydiving at Lodi (sounds like LOW-die) Airport in Acampo, California. When he and Otis got there, the pug made friends with the other skydivers, or jumpers, right away. He did his little circle dance for them. It made them laugh. Some of the jumpers gave Otis treats. Of course, Otis loved that!

Whenever Will went up in a plane with a student, Otis explored the parachute center at the airport. One day, he spied another dog. It was a schnauzer named Jessie. Jessie belonged to the owner of the "drop zone." That's the field where the jumpers land. Otis waited for Will there. Will said that over the years it became "Otis's favorite place to be."

Otis and Jessie loved to hang out together. Sometimes they got into a little trouble. While they were waiting for the skydivers, they got hungry. They sniffed around the backpacks at the drop zone and found the jumpers' lunches. Sometimes Otis helped himself to a sandwich—or two.

Otis became "a regular" out at the airport—just like Will. Skydiving wasn't just Will's job. It was what he loved. His first skydive was right after high school to celebrate his graduation. New skydivers don't jump alone. They are strapped to the front of an experienced skydiver. They share a parachute. This is called a "tandem" jump. Will loved skydiving right away. He wanted to jump by himself.

He's been skydiving ever since that first time. He has made over 13,000 jumps!

Will knew that dogs skydive for the military. They jump into hard-to-reach areas to spy on the enemy or sniff for bombs. That gave Will an idea.

"I'm thinking about taking Otis for a jump," he said to his skydiving pals one day. "What do you think?"

"Sure, go for it," they said.

"What do you think, Otis?" Will asked. Otis wagged his curly tail. "OK," said Will. "I think that means yes!"

The military uses big dogs, like German shepherds. They are strapped to the soldier across the soldier's chest, forming a *t*. But Otis was small. Will thought the pug could be strapped to his chest upright, like a kangaroo in its mother's pouch. It

would be like a beginner's tandem jump. It would feel like true skydiving.

But first Otis needed the right equipment. Will took Otis to meet a master parachute maker named Pete Swan. "Do you think you could make a special harness for Otis?" Will asked.

"Sure," Pete said. Pete designed a harness that strapped Otis to Will's chest, with his head under Will's chin. The pup's front paws were free. He and Will would use the same parachute for the jump. Will just hoped Otis wouldn't try to eat the parachute first!

Otis also needed something to protect his eyes from the wind. So Will took him to the pet store. Will bought Otis a special pair of doggy goggles. Doggy goggles let dogs do other sports too, such as waterskiing.

Will waited until Otis was around a year old to take him on his first jump. It would be a "hop-and-pop." That's a jump from a low height—only 3,000 feet (914 m). Low? That's like jumping off a very tall skyscraper! But it's low for a skydiver. Ten seconds after jumping, Will would open, or pop, the parachute. Then they would float for three to five minutes.

Will picked a bright, sunny day. He put on his own harness. He attached Otis's new harness to his front. He slipped the pup in. Then Will slid the goggles on Otis. Otis looked pretty cool. They would strap on their parachute in the plane.

Jumping for the Military

During World War II, dogs helped the army. Some of them were trained as messengers. Some carried supplies. But some jumped out of planes. They were called "parapups." These dogs parachuted into hard-to-reach areas. Sometimes they were strapped to their handlers. Sometimes they jumped by themselves. The dogs helped track down lost soldiers whose planes crashed in snowy, icy areas near the North Pole. Then they pulled them on sleds to safety. Soldiers say that the dogs wagged their tails the whole time!

In no time, the plane reached the height for their jump. Will and Otis stood at the open door of the plane. *Whoosh!* The air rushed past them. Otis looked around nervously. He squirmed in his harness. *I don't know about this,* he seemed to be thinking. But Will knew that all first-time skydivers are a little scared. He took a deep breath and jumped.

The minute they left the plane, Otis's tongue came out. His ears blew back. He looked around at the scenery. He was like a dog "sticking his head out of the car window," says Will. When they landed, Otis jumped out of his harness and ran around in circles. He wanted a treat, of course!

Not long after their first jump, Will decided to take Otis on another one. He wondered if the pug would be afraid to get into his harness this time. But Otis climbed right in. This time they did a full jump—from 13,000 feet (3,962 m) in the air! That was more than four times higher than Otis's first jump.

Soon Otis was hooked on skydiving, just like Will. As soon as Will brought out his harness, Otis hopped in. Sometimes Otis got *too* excited. Will says, "The hardest part was teaching Otis not to jump into the airplane without his gear on!"

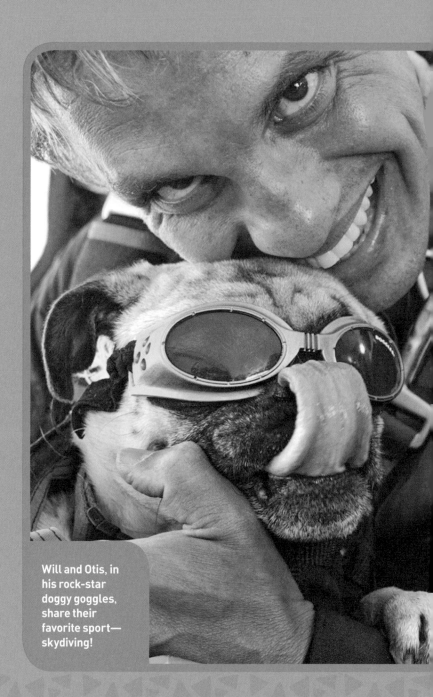

Will and Otis, in his rock-star doggy goggles, share their favorite sport— skydiving!

Chapter 3

Famous FLYER!

Otis couldn't get enough of skydiving. But Will had work to do. He taught new students how to skydive. He filmed other jumpers. Sometimes he even flew the plane. He couldn't take Otis with him every time.

One day, Will was going on a jump without Otis. Otis pawed at him. *Please take me,* the pug seemed to beg. "Not this time, Otis," Will told the pup. As the plane started down the runway, Will looked out the window. He couldn't believe his eyes. Otis was chasing the plane! He didn't want to be left behind—he wanted to jump!

Will saw how much Otis liked meeting other jumpers and how much they liked meeting Otis. "Otis," he said to the pug, "let's have a boogie." A boogie isn't a dance. It's a skydivers' party. It usually takes place at the drop zone. Skydivers chat, make friends, and eat snacks. Did someone say snacks? Otis was in!

Otis and Will hosted an "Otis Boogie" at Lodi Airport. Skydivers from all over the area came to meet Otis. They were amazed by the skydiving pug. Pretty soon, more and more people were talking about

Otis. Jumpers started coming from around the world. They called him "king of the drop zone." Otis was famous!

Before long, some jumpers asked Will, "Can I jump with Otis?" Will was always very careful when he took Otis on jumps. He wasn't going to let just anyone skydive with his beloved pug. He only said "yes" to people he trusted. One of those people was a wingsuit jumper named Ed Pawlowski.

Wingsuiting is skydiving in a special kind of suit. The suit is puffy. It has cloth between the legs and cloth between the arms and the body. If you saw one, you might think of a bat. Or a flying squirrel! The wingsuit slows the fall. The jumper opens the parachute only at the very end. Ed would strap Otis to his wingsuit.

Will has never been wingsuiting. He watched Otis proudly from the ground. As far as Will knew, Otis was the only dog to ever do a wingsuit dive.

Otis loved all the attention. But fame didn't change him— he still loved food best of all! Wherever there was food and no one looking, Otis was there. He tiptoed by. Poof! Another lunch disappeared!

Then one day Will had a problem with Otis's harness. It didn't fit. He couldn't fasten the straps! Uh-oh. Otis had gobbled down too many treats. He'd stolen too many lunches. The piggy little pug's lifestyle had caught up with him!

Will took Otis to the vet. The vet said the pudgy dog had to lose some weight. That meant no more treats! Will wanted Otis to keep skydiving with him. Most of all, Will wanted to keep Otis healthy. So he put Otis on a diet.

Otis was hungry. He missed his treats. He would dance around by the pantry and beg at the drop zone. But Will and the other jumpers said, "No." Being on a diet was tough. But it was worth it. Little by little, Otis slimmed down.

"OK, boy. Let's see if you can slip into your harness now," Will told his dog. It fit. Hooray! Now Will could take Otis skydiving again.

In 2010, Will and Otis entered a skydiving contest called the Best of the

West. It takes place at Lodi every year. Ten skydivers jump out of a plane. They join hands in the sky to build a circle as fast as they can. That's called a ten-way speed star jump. The fastest group to make the speed star wins. Otis was the only dog in the contest. His group won. He even got a certificate!

Then Otis got a big surprise. One day in August 2011, a news team showed up at Lodi Airport. They had cameras. They had microphones. They had a reporter. It was the local TV show, *Good Day Sacramento*. They were there to film Otis skydiving. He was going to be a TV star!

The weather was hot, but the sky was clear. Planes took off. Skydivers jumped. Colorful parachutes appeared in the blue sky.

Summertime Dog Care

Dogs sweat through their paws. They also pant to cool themselves down. It's harder for pugs to cool down because they have such short snouts. They need special care in hot weather. But all dogs need to be watched carefully in the summer. Here are some hot weather tips:

- Never leave a dog alone in a car with the windows up, even for a minute.
- Walk dogs on grass instead of hot cement sidewalks or streets.
- Always have plenty of water for dogs to drink.

They looked like mini rainbows. The reporter watched from the drop zone as jumper after jumper landed.

"Is that him?" the reporter asked. Will's daughter, Nicole, was there that day. She shook her head "no." Then she pointed to a blue-striped parachute.

"That's my dad," she said. And Otis, of course. Pretty soon Will and Otis landed on the ground—a perfect landing.

"Otis was on the top of his A-game that day," said Will. He meant Otis had done his best.

When they reached the ground, Otis leaped out of his harness. He shook himself. He ran around in circles. Then he sat down in front of the camera looking like, well, the star that he was!

Otis's jump was shown on TV. He became more famous than ever. But Otis was getting older. He got tired more easily. Will decided that it was time for the skydiving pug to retire. Otis didn't seem to mind. As long as he could still hang out with Will and Nicole—and get treats!—he was happy.

Someday Will may get another dog. But he doesn't plan to take it skydiving. That was just for Otis. Otis was his "once in a lifetime dog."

Mudslinger shows off his Frisbee skills while an audience looks on.

MUDSLINGER: HAMMING IT UP!

At bedtime, Mudslinger loves to wedge himself between the other pigs.

Chapter 1

PIGS in a BLANKET

One winter day in 2007, John Vincent hung up the phone and turned to his wife, Debbie. "He sounds perfect," he told her. "They're flying him out tomorrow."

John wasn't talking about a person. The passenger he would be meeting at the airport in Denver, Colorado, was a six-month-old potbellied pig.

John had been on the phone with someone from the Pig Placement Network in New York City. It's a rescue group that finds new homes for unwanted pigs. This pig's former owners lived in an apartment. They found out that they couldn't keep a pig there. So they put it up for adoption.

John had seen a picture of the young pig on the Internet. He called to find out more about it. He learned that the pig was very outgoing. The rescue group worker told John that they sometimes took the pig to visit sick people in hospitals. The pig had to ride on elevators, which can be scary for a lot of animals. But this little pig just walked right on.

"That told me he was confident," John said. "I knew I wanted him."

The next day, John drove to the airport in Denver to meet the pig. It was in a pet travel crate. John knew that even the most confident animal can get nervous on an airplane. So he did everything he could to keep the pig relaxed. He slowly wheeled the crate right up to his van. He slid open the van door. Then he opened the crate door. The young pig walked right into the van, as if he knew he belonged there!

John and the pig took a long look at each other. The pig was very cute. He was all pink, with tiny black markings on his face. Like other potbellied pigs, he had a straight tail and small ears.

Then the pig surprised John. He flopped down and rolled onto his side. That meant he was comfortable with John already. It also meant he wanted his belly scratched. John rubbed his tummy.

He knew this little piggy was a keeper. "Come on, little fellow," he said. "We're going home." John named the pig Mudslinger.

John lived on a ranch in Franktown, Colorado. He had always loved animals. He had owned dogs for ages. Then about 20 years ago, some friends told him to think about getting a pet pig. *A pig?* John wasn't sure. But he went to take a look at some potbellied piglets.

The piglets squirmed. They squealed. And they snuffled their flat little snouts, or noses, over everything. Pigs, which are also known as hogs, use their snouts to dig in the ground. That's how they find food.

Potbellied Profile

Potbellied pigs are originally from Vietnam. They usually weigh between 80 and 160 pounds (36 and 73 kg). That's smaller than most American or European farm pigs. Like all pigs, potbellies have no sweat glands. So they wallow in mud or water to stay cool. They mostly eat grains, veggies, and sometimes fruit. Though they can be shy at first, potbellied pigs are social animals. They bond easily with humans and are known to especially love belly rubs!

John fell in love with the wiggly piggies. He brought one home and named him Bacon.

John and Bacon got along so well that John decided to get another potbellied pig. Over the years, John's pig family grew. By the time John brought Mudslinger home, Bacon had passed away, but there were four other potbellied pigs at the ranch. Their names were Pork Chop, Hoover, Peewee, and Zorro. These pigs lived inside John's house, with him and his wife, Debbie. That's where Mudslinger would live, too.

Before John introduced Mudslinger to the other potbellied pigs, he wanted him to feel comfortable in the house. He took him into the living room. Many pigs are fearful in new places. But not Mudslinger. He pranced right in. He looked around. Then he looked at John. John said he could almost hear Mudslinger say, *This will do.*

Now it was time to meet the family. John let the other pigs into the living room. He watched them all closely. Certain pigs are bosses. Sometimes a boss pig can push a little one into a corner and hurt it. Young pigs usually stay away from the big boss hogs.

Mudslinger amazed him again. "Mudslinger was friendly," John said. "He didn't start any fights. He fit right in." The other pigs seemed to like Mudslinger right away. In no time, he became part of John's potbellied pig family.

Even though the potbellies lived in John's house, they didn't eat in the dining room with him and his wife. John had built the pigs their own room for mealtimes. Pigs are clean animals, but they are messy eaters. And they like to eat a lot. At feeding time, Pork Chop, Hoover, Peewee, and Zorro could be, well, piggy. They had poor manners. Some of them would shove the others away from their bowls. They hogged the food. But not Mudslinger. He was a little gentleman right from the start.

The potbellies also had their own bedroom inside the house. It was piled high with blankets. When it was cold, the pigs snuggled into the blankets and covered themselves up. All you could see were their snouts sticking out.

At bedtime, Mudslinger climbed right into the pile of pigs and blankets. He wasn't shy. He didn't sleep at the end of the row. No, that poised (sounds like POYZD) little pig walked across the backs of the bigger pigs. He squirmed and wormed and wiggled his way in. Soon he was wedged between two pigs. Then he nodded off to sleep. John smiled. He nicknamed Mudslinger the "wedge" hog.

Did You Know?

Pigs weigh about 2.5 pounds (1.1 kg) at birth. Some kinds grow up to weigh 700 pounds (300 kg) or more.

Mudslinger uses his super-sensitive snout to check the mail.

PIGHEADED

John was not only a pig lover; he was also a pig trainer. It all started when he got his first pig, Bacon. "I thought people were going to make fun of me for having a pet pig," John said. "So I started training him because I wanted my pig to be better than their dogs."

John trained Bacon like he would train a dog. He praised him.

He gave him dog biscuits. It worked. "It seemed like Bacon learned faster than my dogs did," said John.

Soon John became interested in animal training. He read books about it. He went to a class. Then he took classes with experts. Before long, John was an expert, too.

Maybe I should put together a little show, John thought. It would be fun. And people could see how clever his pigs were. He decided to call his troupe (sounds like TROOP) of little hams "Top Hogs." The show became a hit. Soon, John and his potbellies were performing all over the country.

John hoped that Mudslinger could join the Top Hogs. But before he started training him, he wanted to give the young pig time to get used to his new life. There was one thing Mudslinger needed to learn right away, however. Even though John's pigs ate and slept inside the house, the bathroom was outside!

John's house had a special "hog door," so the pigs could let themselves out. All they had to do was push through the door whenever they needed to go to the bathroom or wanted to lounge on the porch. But to come back in, the pigs had to put their noses behind the handle on the door. Then they could pull it open, just like a "people" door, and squeeze in. John would need to teach Mudslinger how to do that—or so he thought.

When the other pigs went outside, Mudslinger followed them through the hog door. John went out, too, to see what Mudslinger would do. When a pig opened the door to go back in, Mudslinger watched closely. Then he walked up to the door, pulled it open with his nose, and strolled in. Mudslinger had taught himself!

It was clear that Mudslinger was a superfast learner. So John decided to start training him right away. "I didn't want to hold him back," he said.

John took Mudslinger into the living room. That's where he trained all his pigs. John started by giving the pig a treat—a bite of banana or apple, or a grape. Next, John said, "Good," and handed Mudslinger another treat. He did this over and over. Soon, Mudslinger learned that "good" meant a treat.

Smart as a Pig

Have you ever heard that pigs are smarter than dogs? While scientists don't know that for sure, they do know that pigs are extremely intelligent. Pigs learn very quickly, and often on the first try. In fact, studies show that pigs learn some tasks as quickly as chimpanzees. Pigs are also similar to humans. Like us, pigs are able to think through problems and find clever solutions. In one study, pigs were able to use mirrors to find food that had been hidden out of sight!

Now Mudslinger was ready to learn his first trick. John taught it to him one step at a time. First he held a stick up to Mudslinger. He wanted the pig to touch it with his nose. Sometimes it takes a little while for an animal to do what John wants. Not Mudslinger.

He figured it out right away. He pressed his snout to the stick. John said, "Good," and gave him a treat.

Next John tried to get Mudslinger to take a step to touch the stick. When he did, John said, "Good." He handed Mudslinger a grape. Treat by treat, he led the pig around in a circle.

The next step for Mudslinger was to learn to do something on cue. Right before John thought Mudslinger was going to sit, he said, "Sit." Then he rewarded him when he did it. Pretty soon Mudslinger knew what to do when John said, "Sit."

John had Mudslinger practice his tricks in different places. They practiced at different times of the day and in a different order. John needed to know that Mudslinger could do the tricks wherever the show went.

John trained Mudslinger six days a week, like an Olympic athlete. He knew that Mudslinger really wanted to learn. How did he know? Mudslinger told John by his behavior.

Mudslinger was always kind to the other pigs—unless one of them came into the living room during his training time. Then, SQUEAL! Mudslinger grunted and snorted and ran at the other pig. He chased him right out of the room! Mudslinger wanted to learn, and no pig was going to stop him.

Some people might call Mudslinger "pigheaded." Pigs have a reputation for being stubborn. But John thinks that they are just being cautious (sounds like CAW-shus).

Mudslinger was especially good at problem solving. One time, John tried to teach him how to push a golf ball into a ring on the ground. Mudslinger couldn't get the ball over the edge of the ring. But he knew what John wanted. So he picked up the ring and placed it around the ball!

Mudslinger wasn't in training all the time. Like the other potbellies on the ranch, he was a pet. John and Mudslinger cuddled. They touched noses. They slurped ice cream together almost every night.

One day John went looking for his sweatshirt. "Debbie, have you seen it?" he asked his wife. He searched all over the house. Finally, he checked the pigs' bedroom. Sure enough, Mudslinger had taken it. He had placed it on top of the pile of blankets. *Sweet dreams, little piggy.*

Mudslinger toots his own horn at a Top Hogs show. The little pig loves to perform.

Chapter 3

Mudslinger learned tricks faster than any other pig John had trained. After only two months, he was ready to be in the Top Hogs show.

At first, John had Mudslinger perform small tricks. But in no time, the pig was ready for harder tricks. In one trick, Mudslinger put his mouth up to a microphone. He pretended to be singing an Elvis song. The audience laughed. Then he raised an American flag with his snout. The audience applauded.

In another trick, John held up a hoop. He motioned for Mudslinger to jump through it. Mudslinger gave John a funny look. He seemed to say, *No way.* Then he stretched his neck. He took the hoop in his mouth and lowered it to the stage. He *walked* through!

Later in the act, Mudslinger hopped on a skateboard. Another pig pushed him across the stage. *Grind on, Tony Hawg!*

Has Mudslinger ever had stage fright? Only once. John always takes the animals on the stage before a performance. He wants them to feel comfortable when it's showtime. They look around. They walk across the stage. One time, Mudslinger walked onstage and froze. John was never sure what happened. He thinks Mudslinger saw a shadow and became afraid. So far it hasn't happened again.

Mudslinger was less than a year old when he was invited to be on TV. National Geographic was making a show called *Brilliant Beasts* that would tell stories about smart pigeons, dogs, and hogs. They had heard about the pig prodigy (sounds like PRAH-duh-gee) and wanted to feature him in an episode called *Hog Genius*.

Mudslinger never missed a cue. The filmmaker said that he had never seen a pig do everything it was asked to do. When it was time to film Mudslinger, he would joke, "Time for another slingshot!"

Kids Can Help

John Vincent adopted Mudslinger through the Pig Placement Network (PPN). PPN workers rescue unwanted or abandoned pet potbellied pigs. Then they help find them loving new homes. You can also help homeless pigs and other animals. Here are some ways:

- Volunteer to clean cages at shelters.
- Help collect food and supplies for shelters.
- Organize a penny drive. Set up jars or cans at school. Ask people to donate pennies. Send the money to an animal rescue group.

Always check with your parents first, and ask at the animal shelter about helping.

Soon after that, Mudslinger was invited to be on another TV show. This time it was an animal talent contest. John and Mudslinger trotted out onstage.

"Wave hello to everybody," said John. Mudslinger waved his foot.

"Now play dead." Mudslinger rolled onto his side.

John threw a toy. "Fetch this for me." Mudslinger brought it back. Then Mudslinger lifted the lid of a toy box with his nose. He dropped the toy in.

Finally, John set up a soccer goal. He put orange cones in a row. It was Mudslinger's hardest trick. "I want to see you move in and out," he told Mudslinger. Mudslinger pushed the soccer ball around each cone.

"I hope he has a nose for the goal," John said. Mudslinger gave the ball a shove. It hit the goalpost. "Aaawwww," said someone in the audience. But he didn't know Mudslinger. That pig didn't give up. He pushed the ball one more time. Goal!

Mudslinger won the talent contest. The host tried to put a medal on him. But Mudslinger wasn't interested. The host put it on John instead.

The little ham was becoming quite famous. In 2010, he took another step on his road to stardom. A major TV network was hosting an even bigger pet talent contest. Pet stars from all around the nation were invited to compete. Mudslinger was one of them.

The show's producers flew John and Mudslinger to New York City. They put them up in a fancy hotel. Did Mudslinger go hog wild and call for room service? No, but the little porker and John did enjoy their nightly ice cream.

The next day was the show. Mudslinger competed against four other talented animals. There was a bird that played golf and a dog that played cards. There was a water-skiing squirrel and a dog that jumped rope. But Mudslinger was a trouper. He did his tricks perfectly, just like always. And he won! But that was just the first round of the contest.

Did You Know?

Pigs have four toes on each foot. But they only walk on two, so they look like they are on their tiptoes.

A little while later, John and Mudslinger came back to New York to compete in the finals. While they were there, they visited the Pig Placement Network. The lady who had rescued Mudslinger was happy to see him doing so well.

Then John and Mudslinger went to the TV studio for the big event. Mudslinger beat all the other animals again! He was declared the most talented pet in America. He has the trophy (sounds like TRO-fee) to prove it!

These days Mudslinger and the other Top Hogs perform at schools, libraries, county fairs, and rodeos all over the country. Mudslinger hardly ever makes a mistake onstage. But he can get carried away. John has an instrument he calls a "hogs-a-phone." It's a stand with bicycle horns of different sizes and sounds.

The pigs play their own songs on it. When this musical performance is over, John moves the hogs-a-phone to the back of the stage. But sometimes Mudslinger isn't finished. He tiptoes to the back of the stage and makes more music!

Some research suggests that math and musical talent go together. That's true for Mudslinger. He now knows an amazing math trick. John sets up five cups. Each cup has a number from one to five painted on it. John lines them up in order by number.

He asks Mudslinger, "What is one plus two?" He uses his fingers to help ask the question. Mudslinger walks along the cups, stops, and picks up the cup marked "3." He brings it to John.

Then John asks him, "Mudslinger, what's two plus three?" Mudslinger walks in front of the cups again. He looks at them carefully. He pauses by cup number three, but moves on. Finally, he picks up cup number five.

There's no doubt about it: Mudslinger is one brainy hog. John knew from day one that the little pig was hungry to learn. He still is. So what's next for Mudslinger? Algebra?

THE END

INDEX

MORE INFORMATION

To find more information about the animal species featured in this book, check out these articles and websites:

"Doggy daring takes Otis skydiving," the *Sacramento Bee* (newspaper article and video)
www.sacbee.com/2011/08/16/3840235/doggy-daring-takes-otis-skydiving.html

Knoxville Zoo website
www.knoxville-zoo.org/animals_attractions/animal_guide/birds/congo_african_grey_parrot.aspx

National Geographic "Animals: Domestic Dog"
animals.nationalgeographic.com/animals/mammals/domestic-dog

National Geographic "Animals: Parrot"
animals.nationalgeographic.com/animals/birds/parrot

National Geographic "Creature Features: Pigs"
kids.nationalgeographic.com/kids/animals/creaturefeature/pigs

Top Hogs: Family-Fun Performances website
www.tophogs.com

**This book is dedicated to
a superstar in my life, my Aunt Joan. —MRD**

CREDITS

ACKNOWLEDGMENTS

My heartfelt thanks to:

My editor, Marfé Ferguson Delano, who taught me so much about
strong verbs, strong story, and great writing; Will da Silva, skydiving companion of Otis, for his generosity in sharing Otis's story;
Tina Rolen, Teresa Collins, and Nikki Edwards at the Knoxville Zoo
in Tennessee for their expertise and help in introducing me to
Einstein's world (and a special thanks to Einstein for speaking to
me on the phone!); John Vincent, owner and trainer of Mudslinger,
for his extraordinary help; Paige Towler, for her pig sidebars; and
as always, my family for their help and support in every way.

APE ESCAPES!

And More True Stories of Animals Behaving Badly

Aline Alexander Newman

Published by the National Geographic Society
John M. Fahey, Jr., *Chairman of the Board and Chief Executive Officer*
Timothy T. Kelly, *President*
Declan Moore, *Executive Vice President; President, Publishing and Digital Media*
Melina Gerosa Bellows, *Executive Vice President; Chief Creative Officer, Books, Kids, and Family*

Prepared by the Book Division
Hector Sierra, *Senior Vice President and General Manager*
Nancy Laties Feresten, *Senior Vice President, Editor in Chief, Children's Books*
Jonathan Halling, *Design Director, Books and Children's Publishing*
Jay Sumner, *Director of Photography, Children's Publishing*
Jennifer Emmett, *Editorial Director, Children's Books*
Eva Absher-Schantz, *Managing Art Director, Children's Books*
Carl Mehler, *Director of Maps*
R. Gary Colbert, *Production Director*
Jennifer A. Thornton, *Director of Managing Editorial*

Staff for This Book
Becky Baines, *Project Editor*
Lisa Jewell, *Illustrations Editor*
Eva Absher, *Art Director*
Ruthie Thompson, *Designer*
Grace Hill, *Associate Managing Editor*
Joan Gossett, *Production Editor*
Lewis R. Bassford, *Production Manager*
Susan Borke, *Legal and Business Affairs*
Kate Olesin, *Assistant Editor*
Allie Allen, *Design Production Assistant*
Hillary Moloney, *Illustrations Assistant*

Manufacturing and Quality Management
Christopher A. Liedel, *Chief Financial Officer*
Phillip L. Schlosser, *Senior Vice President*
Chris Brown, *Vice President*
George Bounelis, *Vice President, Production Services*
Nicole Elliott, *Manager*
Rachel Faulise, *Manager*
Robert L. Barr, *Manager*

The National Geographic Society is one of the world's largest nonprofit scientific and educational organizations. Founded in 1888 to "increase and diffuse geographic knowledge," the Society works to inspire people to care about the planet. National Geographic reflects the world through its magazines, television programs, films, music and radio, books, DVDs, maps, exhibitions, live events, school publishing programs, interactive media and merchandise. *National Geographic* magazine, the Society's official journal, published in English and 33 local-language editions, is read by more than 38 million people each month. The National Geographic Channel reaches 320 million households in 34 languages in 166 countries. National Geographic Digital Media receives more than 15 million visitors a month. National Geographic has funded more than 9,400 scientific research, conservation, and exploration projects and supports an education program promoting geography literacy. For more information, visit nationalgeographic.com.

For more information, please call
1-800-NGS LINE (647-5463) or
write to the following address:
National Geographic Society
1145 17th Street N.W.
Washington, D.C. 20036-4688 U.S.A.

Visit us online at nationalgeographic.com/books

For librarians and teachers: ngchildrensbooks.org

> National Geographic supports K–12
> educators with ELA Common Core
> Resources. Visit natgeoed.org/
> commoncore for more information.

More for kids from National Geographic:
kids.nationalgeographic.com

For information about special discounts for bulk purchases, please contact National Geographic Books Special Sales:
ngspecsales@ngs.org

For rights or permissions inquiries, please contact National Geographic Books Subsidiary Rights: ngbookrights@ngs.org

Trade paperback ISBN: 978-1-4263-0936-6
Reinforced library edition ISBN:
978-1-4263-0955-7

Table of CONTENTS

Fu is a 250-pound (114 kg) "pasha." A pasha is a full-grown male with cheek pads.

FU MANCHU: APE ESCAPES!

In the wild, baby orangutans like this one stay with their moms eight years or more.

Chapter 1

A SCAMP IS BORN

July 1965, Omaha, Nebraska

A young orangutan peers out of his cage at the Henry Doorly Zoo. No humans are in sight. The coast is clear.

He sticks his long fingers through the chain-link fence. He bends back one corner. He pulls. *ZZIIIIP!* The stiff metal fencing unravels like a hand-knit scarf.

Some time later, veterinarian Lee Simmons arrives at work. He rounds a bend in the path and *yikes!* Dr. Simmons stops in his tracks. It couldn't be, but it is. A shaggy, red-haired ape sits up in a tree. *How did he get loose?*

The ape is about six years old, tailless, and weighs 100 pounds (45 kg). He has a mustache and beard like a famous movie character. For that reason he is called Fu Manchu. Fu's arms are super strong and longer than most fourth graders are tall. In a wrestling match against a man, the orangutan would win.

The ape doesn't move or make a sound. But Dr. Simmons sees a twinkle in his eyes. The vet can't help but wonder if Fu knew what he was doing. *It's like he's been sitting there just waiting for me.*

Fu climbs down. The sun sparkles on his red hair as he scrambles back to his cage. Dr. Simmons follows, shaking his head. *What a crazy ape!* He locks Fu inside. He calls someone to fix the fence and then goes about his normal business. And Fu goes about his—dreaming up more hijinks to come.

Fu was born in a rain forest on the Indonesian island of Sumatra (sounds like SUE-MAH-TRA). Like most baby orangutans, Fu probably never knew his father. Orangutan mothers care for their helpless babies. Fu's mother nursed him. She held him and snuggled him. Every night she built them a nest high in the treetops.

These sleeping nests were the size of

For the first few weeks after they're born, baby orangutans cling to their moms' bellies.

bathtubs. Fu's mother made them by twisting leafy branches together. Each fresh, new nest must have felt as comfy to Fu as clean bedsheets do to you.

Usually Fu and his mom stayed dry in their cozy bed in the sky. At other times thunder boomed. Rain fell in sheets. Then the apes huddled together and turned giant leaves into umbrellas.

During the day, Fu often rode on his mother's back. He clutched her hair as they swung through the trees looking for durian (sounds like DUR-EE-ANN) fruits. Durian fruits stink like sweaty gym socks. But orangutans go ape for the smelly stuff.

The problem is durian fruits don't all

ripen at the same time, and the trees are scattered. To find them, orangutans must keep a map of the forest inside their heads. For Fu's mother it must have been like memorizing a school bus route with hundreds of stops.

Finding water was easier. It collects in hollow tree trunks after a rain. Fu might have gotten a drink by scooping water out with a folded leaf. Or maybe he chewed leaves into a sort of sponge. Then he sopped up water and dripped it into his mouth. Either way, Fu used leaves as tools.

Long ago, Indonesian people dubbed these clever apes "orangutans." In their language the word *orang* means

Did You Know?

As baby orangutans get older, they ride "piggyback" to get a better view of their surroundings.

"person" and *utan* means "forest." Together you get "person of the forest."

One day Fu and his mother heard strange sounds in the swamp. Hunters had entered the jungle. They carried axes and homemade nets on their backs. Rivers of sweat ran down the men's bare chests. Armies of insects buzzed in their faces. But nothing stopped them. The men were animal collectors. They feed their families by catching and selling wild animals. A baby orangutan will get them a lot of money.

Did Fu's mother know they wanted her baby? Probably not, but she sensed danger. She swung from limb to limb, snapping off branches. She threw the branches down on the hunters.

Orangutans and Tools

Orangutans are the smartest of all the great apes. They learn new things quickly. Because of this, people have spent years studying orangutans and learning more about them. Orangutans have been seen in the wild and in zoos using tools to scratch themselves; cover themselves from the rain; collect water, honey, or bugs for food; swat stinging insects; and spear fish in the water.

The animal collectors looked up. The mother ape looked like a tiny black doll hanging against the blue sky. Was she holding a baby?

The hunters had a traditional way of catching orangutans. They didn't try to climb up after them. Not at first. That might have spooked the ape into escaping through the treetops. Instead, the animal collectors formed a circle. They pulled out their axes and hacked away at tree trunks.

The ground shook as a tall tree crashed to the forest floor. Then a second one, and a third. The trees were so close together that each one that fell knocked down another. CHOP! CHOP! The men worked their way to the last tree—the one holding the apes.

"*Pzz squee.*" Fu's mother squeaked and ran, looking for a way to escape. Seeing none, she moved far out on a limb.

A man climbed way, way up the smooth trunk. He broke off a leafy branch and shook it at her.

Fu's mother probably did what most orangutans do when cornered by hunters. She smacked her lips. Her black eyes shone with fear. With one man in the tree and more below, she first scrambled up and then down. Up and then down.

Suddenly the scared ape leaped to the ground. With her baby hugging her belly, she ran for her life. But the men ran faster.

The boss hunter yelled. He ordered his men to throw their nets.

SWOOSH! The apes were trapped!

Fu, always the practical joker, loved performing for happy, smiling zoo visitors.

HERO Prankster

The animal collectors have gotten what they came for. They carry Fu out of the jungle and ship him to Singapore. They put him up for sale in the marketplace. Except for his fur, the little red ape looks much like a human baby. An American man has come to buy animals for a zoo in Louisiana. He likes the look of Fu. The American has already spent a lot of money on rare parrots, monkeys, pythons, and crocodiles. Now he buys Fu.

Fu spends three years in Louisiana. Then he is sent to Omaha, Nebraska.

In the wild, Fu swung from branches and hung from vines. Thumbs on his feet as well as his hands helped him hang on. Sometimes he went two weeks without touching the ground.

Life is different in a zoo. Soon after Fu arrives in Omaha, the zookeepers build a large, modern Great Ape House. But only a few trees grow in the Ape House yard. They are nothing like the giant trees that grow packed together in the rain forest. Fu can't build a sleeping nest in them. There is no tangled jungle for him to learn his way around. But the most important difference is food. Here a zookeeper brings him supper in a bowl. Fu does not need to find his own meals. He does not need to memorize 1,000 different kinds of plants like his mom did.

Like a bored kid in school, Fu turns his mind to other things. When a tree dies in his yard, Fu pulls it apart. He gathers up two chunks of wood and sets them against the building. They make a ramp that he can climb.

"There's an ape on the roof!" shouts a zoo visitor.

Dr. Simmons rushes to the scene. "Fu," he orders, hands on his hips. "Come down from there."

Fu ignores him. The naughty ape scrambles across the roof and wraps his hairy arms around the chimney. CAARACK! He tears it off the roof and flings it over the edge!

That does it. Zookeeper Jerry Stones has had enough. Maybe he can help the bored ape stay out of trouble. He will give Fu something to swing on.

Jerry goes inside the orangutan's cage and hangs a chain from one wall to another. Fu sits quietly in a corner and pretends not to notice, but the tricky ape is secretly watching the whole time.

Looks good, Jerry thinks, when he finishes. He packs up his tools and leaves, banging the door behind him.

The next morning Jerry returns to

Did You Know?

An orangutan has very long arms. Together they stretch more than 7 feet (2 m)!

admire his work. But when he enters the ape house, he just stands there in shock! The steel chain he had so carefully hung lies in a pile on the floor. Fu stands beside it—holding the screws in his fist.

Grumbling, Jerry rehangs the chain. Then he pulls out his hammer. WHAM! He flattens the end of each screw.

Not even Fu can take them out now, he thinks.

A month goes by. Jerry forgets the mischief. He goes to the Ape House to give Fu some monkey biscuits and . . . gasp! The heavy chain lies on the floor like a broken necklace. *How on earth?*

Fu was sneaky. He must have spent weeks turning those screws when no one was looking.

"Doggone it, Fueey," mutters Jerry. He grabs a ladder and tools.

CLATTER! CLANK! BANG! Jerry hangs the chain for the third time.

Fu is naughty all right, but he is also kind. On another day Dr. Simmons and a second man are working together inside Fu's cage. The floor is wet. The other man slips and sticks out his hand to catch himself. He accidentally touches the big picture window that separates Fu from zoo visitors.

ZAP!

An electric shock knocks the man across the room. He lands curled up on the floor.

Fu rushes to help. First, he looks over the shaken man for injuries. Then he straightens out the man's finger. Finally, he leads him to the window.

The window is electrified to keep Fu from smudging the glass. But one little strip is safe to touch, and Fu knows it. The smart ape places the man's finger there. It is like he is saying, "Next time, touch here. Then you won't get hurt."

Fu made zoo officials want more apes like him. But the Indonesian government passed a law protecting orangutans. Catching, killing, and selling them was illegal. That left one solution. They had to find Fu a girl orangutan.

Zookeepers put Fu and another orangutan named "Tondelayo" together. The two apes hit it off right away, but Tondelayo doesn't like Jerry. She paces and her lips tighten whenever he enters their cage. He feels uneasy around her.

One day it happens.

Jerry is feeding Tondelayo when she suddenly sinks her teeth into his leg! She bites through his rubber boot, wool pants, and heavy socks. "Arghh!" Jerry screams. Trying to get away, he whacks Tondelayo in the head with the rubber feed bucket.

She lets go.

With his leg bleeding, Jerry hops to safety.

Fu had done nothing. But weeks later Tondelayo attacks again. This time Fu is ready. He jumps on his mate and bites her hard. Tondelayo squeaks and backs off. She never hurts Jerry again.

If You Give an Ape an iPad...

They finger-paint, watch home videos, and look at books, says Trish Khan. Trish is a zookeeper at Wisconsin's Milwaukee County Zoo. She says orangutans are so intelligent that they need to be introduced to new things. Otherwise they get bored.

Trish thinks someone should design a kind of Facebook app for apes. Using it, an orangutan could touch another ape's photo and watch a live cam of that ape in action.

"The things that interest kids also interest an orangutan," says Khan. Imagine if you could play Flick Kick Football on your phone with an ape!

Once Fu mastered the art of the escape, it was time to teach the other orangutans how to misbehave.

Wise Guy Ape

"Jerry! Jerry! The orangutans are out!"

Jerry Stones is now head zookeeper. He hears the shouts, but it takes a minute for the words to sink in. When they do, he jumps up from his desk and races outside.

"Over there! In the trees." A visitor points to a group of elms on a hill near the elephant barn. It is late fall, and their leaves have dropped. Jerry spots what looks like five big, hairy apes sitting on the bare branches.

Not waiting for help, Jerry scrambles up one of the trees as if he were an ape himself. He takes one orangutan by the hand and leads him back to the Ape House. Jerry does this again and again, until he has everybody back where they belong. Now Jerry must figure out how they escaped.

One thing he knows already. Fu was behind it. He let himself out and then snapped off the padlocks on the other apes' cages. But how did he do it? Jerry checks the Ape House yard for anything strange.

After a while, he looks into a deep ditch that works like a fence. In the bottom, at one end of the ditch, is a door. This door leads into the basement of the Ape House. But it is not an ordinary door. This door is meant to be secure, so it doesn't have an outside handle. It can only be opened from the inside by someone using a key.

But it's open! *Aha!* Jerry thinks. *Some careless keeper forgot to lock it.* He steps inside. The place is a mess. Dirt covers the floor, and there are pipes thrown about. Jerry follows the trail. It leads to a ladder. The apes had climbed up to the first floor. Then they simply pushed open the big glass doors and walked out into the sun.

Jerry warns the keepers. "Do not let this happen again!"

But happen it does—the very next week. And again the week after that!

After the third breakout, Jerry says that he will fire the person who left the door open.

That's when he and a keeper spot Fu in the ditch. Three other apes are gathered around watching over his shoulder. Fu slips a little wire under the lock, and like magic, the door swings open.

The men run into the building and block the apes from coming up the ladder. Jerry takes away Fu's "key" and returns everyone to their cages. "From now on," Jerry says, "keepers will sweep the ditch every day. They'll rake the grass and search under bushes for wires."

He thinks the problem is solved.

Did You Know?

Orangutans in the wild spend up to 90 percent of their time in treetops.

But weeks later, Jerry spots something shiny poking out of Fu's mouth. "Open up, Fueey," Jerry says. Fu does, and Jerry sticks in his finger. He feels around and pulls out guess what. Another piece of wire! The sneaky ape has bent it like a horseshoe to fit in his mouth!

But there's one question left. Where is Fu getting these wires?

One day Dr. Simmons goes to the Ape House. He finds Fu lying on his side reaching through the bars. *Now what's he up to?* Dr. Simmons stays out of sight and watches.

A female orangutan named Heavy Lamar lives next door to Fu. Dr. Simmons has her on a diet because she is too fat. Pretty soon the vet sees Heavy's hairy arm slide from around the corner. She and Fu touch hands, and Fu slips Heavy a monkey biscuit. In return, Heavy gives him a piece of wire. The wire is from a screen that covers the lightbulb hanging in her cage.

They have their answer.

Jerry and his crew scurry around securing the Ape House. They screw steel plates on the doors to the orangutan cages. That way Fu can't twist off the locks. They smooth out the sides of the ditch so no orangutan can climb it. They fix the light screen in Heavy's cage.

This time their work pays off. The ape escapes stop.

Lovable Fu is a 250-pound (114 kg) "pasha" now. Pashas are full-grown males and have cheek flaps and a big throat pouch. The throat pouch helps Fu make the "long call." This is a sound that can be heard from over a mile (1.6 km) away.

As big as Fu is, Bornean (sounds like BORE-NEE-ANN) orangutans grow even larger. The males have even bigger cheek flaps. In 1983, the Omaha zoo had Bornean and Sumatran orangutans. The people in charge later decided to focus on just one kind—the Bornean apes. Because Fu is from Sumatra, they sent him to the Gladys Porter Zoo in Texas.

In Texas, Fu becomes a big shot all over again—but for another reason. He is the only male in a group of females. Before his death in 1992, Fu fathered twenty babies. So far, none of them has pulled any such silly stunts as their father did. But who knows? One of them still might.

Orangutan Friends

In the wild, orangutans usually live alone. But they occasionally get together in groups, and mom orangutans spend years raising their young (unlike many other animals). Scientists think that this means they live alone because they have to. In the wild, their food is scattered and hard to find. Orangutans in groups would have a harder time getting enough to eat. In zoos, orangutans seem to not mind each other's company. Fu and Heavy were friends and even helped each other.

Some people wonder. *Did Fu's many escapes mean he hated zoo life?* Probably not. The mischief-loving ape ate good meals. He could go inside out of the rain to be warm and dry. He seemed to enjoy playing in his yard, helping raise his babies, and showing off for visitors.

But there is stronger proof. No matter how many times Fu broke out of his cage, he never left the zoo grounds. The clever ape always came back.

Maybe Fu never intended to run away. Maybe he liked using his brain and simply enjoyed playing jokes.

Curtis and Peggy sit together on a hill near their home in the United Kingdom.

PEGGY: THE MISCHIEVOUS PUP

Peggy loves to jump. Here she jumps for a stick that Curtis tries to hold out of her reach.

Chapter 1

**April 2007,
Northumberland, England**

Peggy the mutt lifts her black, wet nose in the air. *Sniff! Sniff!* Something smells yummy! She jumps to her feet and runs into the kitchen. The lady of the house has just pulled a baked ham out of the oven.

Peggy flops down in the middle of the tiny room. The busy woman almost trips over her. "Go away,

Peggy!" she orders. "This isn't for you."
But Peggy stays. Every little while, she
inches closer to the prize. A puddle of dog
drool forms on the floor.

Suddenly *BRR-IIING! BRR-IIING!*
The telephone rings. The lady forgets about
Peggy and hurries to answer it.

Big mistake.

The waiting dog grabs the ham as quick
as a frog catching a fly. Two gulps and it's
gone! Every last bit! Full and happy, Peggy
lies down and licks her mouth.

This doesn't please the woman's hungry
family. They have only bread and veggies
for dinner!

Peggy belongs to Tony and Lorraine
Shaw and their sons, Daniel, six, and
Curtis, seven. Mr. Shaw rescued Peggy

from an old junkyard. Now they all live together in a three-bedroom house beside the North Sea. Curtis loves the mutt and plays with her a lot. But even he admits she's naughty—has been ever since his dad brought her home. Take the problem with the laundry, for example.

Mrs. Shaw used to hang her wash on the line. One day Peggy ran, jumped, and tore it down. Wooden clothes-pegs flew through the air as Peggy yanked down shirts, pants, and underwear. *Snap! Snap!* More clothes dropped. More pegs popped. In minutes, all the wash lay on the ground. Why? Peggy loved to chew on the pegs.

"Bad dog," Mrs. Shaw said.

The guilty puppy stopped chewing. She lowered her head and laid back her ears. Her eyelids drooped. She didn't mean to be bad.

But what happened the next time Mrs. Shaw hung out wet clothes? The little rascal yanked them down again. Mrs. Shaw saw the mess and sighed. She put her hands on her hips.

"If you like clothes-pegs this much," she said, "that's what we'll name you—Peggy."

The floppy-eared, black and brown troublemaker is part Rottweiler and part German shepherd. Her paws are big as plates. "She is soft all over like a teddy bear," says Curtis. But the best thing about her? She makes him laugh.

The gleeful sound of Curtis laughing

brightens the entire Shaw household. It especially makes Mr. and Mrs. Shaw happy. Curtis has many health problems. He can't eat snacks made with eggs or nuts because his throat will swell shut. Sometimes he finds it hard to breathe. There is also something different about Curtis's brain that makes his mind wander. He doesn't listen well. He squirms in his seat, and he talks too loud. This makes him a target for bullies.

Before Peggy came, Curtis often acted angry or sad. He didn't have many friends.

Now he has a buddy in Peggy. At home she follows him everywhere. She listens to everything he says and never argues or talks back. As Mr. Shaw explains, "She just loves Curtis to bits." But guess what?

Peggy may be the world's naughtiest dog.

Her stunts can be silly or serious. Peggy jumps up on people. Curtis yells and tries to stop her. But he might as well try to stop a speeding train. Peggy gets so excited when visitors come to the house that she charges into them. She only wants to say hello, but sometimes she knocks people flat. If she gets really excited, she loses control and pees on their feet.

"Sorry," says Curtis.

"Ewww," say the visitors.

Everyone living with Peggy must pick up their things. Besides clothes-pegs, she chews on soccer balls. She sneaks upstairs and eats the stuffing out of teddy bears. She even chews on table legs. From socks to spider plants, the Shaws follow one rule. "Put it up high or say goodbye!"

When Peggy isn't chewing, she's barking. She barks at strangers. She barks at birds. She barks at most anything that moves.

And that's not all she does. Peggy eats so much that she grows faster than Pinocchio's nose. She gobbles the food Curtis pours in her dish. Then she pokes her head into the bag looking for more. She eats frozen peas out of the package and smelly garbage in the trash can. Her worst food prank is still stealing the ham.

After pigging out on the family's supper that night, Peggy snuffles around wanting a cuddle. Curtis doesn't feel like cuddling. He'd rather have ham. The puppy paws at his knee. Curtis looks away. She pushes her head under his hand and cries for attention. "I'm mad at you," Curtis says. The puppy puts her paws on his shoulders. *Slurp.*

Curtis giggles and wipes his chin.

"Oh, all right," he says and pulls her into his lap.

But minutes later . . . "Pee-yew!" Curtis pulls his shirt up over his nose. Eating people food makes Peggy pass gas.

Curtis waves at the air. "Bad dog," he grumbles.

Peggy grins and thumps her tail on the floor.

Mr. and Mrs. Shaw can't help themselves. They love the goofy mutt. So does Daniel. Curtis loves her most of all. But one day Peggy's troublemaking goes too far. You might even say it "takes the cake."

All About Dogs

1. All dogs descend from wolves.
2. A 6.6-pound (3 kg) Chihuahua named Momo is the world's smallest search and rescue dog.
3. A dog's nose print is as individual as a human's fingerprint.
4. Dogs are the most varied species. They come in hundreds of shapes and sizes.
5. Chaser the Border collie may be the world's smartest dog. He knows the names of more than 1,000 objects.
6. A Labrador retriever–poodle mix is called a Labradoodle.
7. "Trouble," a white Maltese, is richer than most people. He inherited $12 million.

Peggy and Mrs. Shaw show off the biggest mess Peggy ever made.

Chapter 2

EMERGENCY!

I t's Mr. Shaw's 46th birthday. To celebrate, Mrs. Shaw buys a chocolate cake. White icing spells out "Happy Birthday" across the top. The baker packs the cake in a bakery box, and Mrs. Shaw carries it home. The Shaw family must wait to enjoy it later. They are due at school for a meeting with Curtis's teacher.

Mrs. Shaw hunts for a hiding place in her small kitchen. Finally she tucks the cake on a shelf high above the stove. *Peggy will never get it up here,* she figures. Then she hears a buzzer. The laundry is done. Mrs. Shaw bends down and pulls a pile of warm towels out of the dryer. She dumps them on the counter next to the stove.

"Come on, boys," she says. "Let's go."

Curtis pushes Peggy off his lap. "Be a good dog," he says. "We won't be gone long."

The whole family heads out the door. Mr. Shaw leaves last. He turns the bolt and tugs the door to make sure it's locked. They will stop at his mother's house on the way. Nana will watch the kids while he and Mrs. Shaw go to the meeting.

No sooner does the family leave than Peggy follows her nose into the kitchen.

Mrs. Shaw hid the cake, but "out of sight, out of mind" does not work for dogs. Peggy sniffs everything, and her brain is one big filing cabinet full of odors. Her sense of smell is so powerful that she knows people, places, and animals by scent—not by their looks. Now Peggy smells cake!

She jumps for it like she jumps for clothes-pegs. One big leap and Peggy knocks the cake down with her snout. She also accidentally moves the pile of towels. Some of them land on a stove burner. Does Peggy also bump the knob and turn the burner on? Or did Mrs. Shaw forget to turn it off in her hurry to leave? It doesn't matter. Minutes pass. Smoke rises from the pile of towels. Then . . .

FIRE!

Red and orange flames shoot toward the ceiling. They crackle and hiss. Thick black smoke chokes the air. It makes it hard for Peggy to breathe. *Woof! Woof! Ayyoooo!* She howls for help.

Peggy's cries alert the man living on the other side of their two-family house. He comes over to see what's wrong and discovers the fire.

The neighbor runs home. "Call the fire department!" he yells to his wife. Then he hurries back to try and save Peggy. He grabs the back door handle and pulls. "Oh, no!" The door is locked!

The neighbor cups his hands around his

eyes and looks through a window. He can't see a thing in the smoke-filled house. He bangs on the glass with his fist. "Peggy! Come, Peggy!" he calls.

But Peggy doesn't come.

Minutes later, the Shaws arrive at Nana's house. Mr. Shaw's cell phone rings. He flips it open. "Hello."

"Tony! Your house . . . Your house is on fire!" his neighbor yells.

Our house is on fire? The news is so shocking that Mr. Shaw can't take it in. He starts to ask a question, but the neighbor interrupts.

"Peggy is in there," he says. "She's howling and screaming, and I can't get her out. The door is locked. Oh, Tony, it's dreadful to hear."

"Hold on. We're coming."

Mr. Shaw tells his wife and mother the awful news. The kids are out of the room and cannot hear. "Go," Nana says. "I'll watch the boys." Mr. and Mrs. Shaw jump into their car and speed toward home.

Meanwhile, heat and smoke are still building up inside their house. A red fire truck arrives on the scene with its siren screaming. Two firefighters leap to the ground and race toward the house. *Are people trapped inside?* A fireman smashes through the door with an ax. Then in they go, dragging a fire hose.

The firemen can see the stove in the light from the flames. *Sploosh!* They spray it with water. The flames die down. Now the smoke makes it dark as night. The firemen find their way by touch. They make a map of doorways and chairs in their heads so they can get back out.

First they climb the stairs and search the bedrooms. There's no one there. They go back through the living room and into the bathroom. Firefighter Martin Kammeier feels around for the toilet and sink. He puts his hand in the tub. Whoa! He feels something. It's soft and furry.

It's a dog!

What is a dog doing in the bathtub? Martin realizes she was trying to breathe through the drain. Poor Peggy. She doesn't know that the U-shaped pipe connection to the drain prevents gases—and fresh air—from entering the house.

Martin searches some more. Nothing.

He carries Peggy outside. She is limp as a noodle, and her tongue is hanging out. He drops her motionless body on the ground and runs back into the house. He has to finish putting out the fire.

Firefighter Stephen Buglass is outside setting up medical equipment in case it is needed. Stephen is a highly trained emergency worker. He once belonged to the best rescue team in all of England. The trouble is he usually works on humans. He does not expect to be handed a dog.

Stephen knows most fire victims do not die of burns. They die from breathing in smoke. Peggy spent over ten minutes inside the burning house. Her lungs must be full of deadly ash. The firefighter doubts he can save her. He thinks it's hopeless.

Trust the Nose

Dogs have super noses. Their sense of smell is 100,000 times better than a human's. To understand how good that is, imagine an Olympic-size swimming pool full of water. Then imagine stirring in a spoonful of sugar. A dog could smell the difference.

Specially trained dogs can sniff out bombs, drugs, harmful mold, and bedbugs. They can track down criminals and find missing kids.

Now dogs are learning to smell sickness. They can tell if people have cancer by smelling their breath. That's right. Your lovable pooch may be a doctor on four legs.

Peggy sits in the burnt bathtub where she was found during the fire.

Chapter 3

Firefighter Stephen Buglass looks at the oxygen mask in his equipment. The mask is designed for people and doesn't fit a dog's pointy face. He pulls off the mask and sticks its tube down the dog's throat. His partner turns on the oxygen and holds the tube in place.

Stephen places one hand over the other and pushes up and down on the dog's heart. This is hard work. Beads of sweat form on Stephen's forehead as he pushes almost 100 times a minute. A small crowd gathers to watch. Everyone wonders the same thing. Will the sweet-looking puppy come back to life?

Ten minutes pass. Twenty. Thirty. The fireman's arms feel heavy. He can't pump this dog's heart much longer. The animal hasn't moved. Stephen is ready to quit.

Then he notices something. It can't be. But it is! Inside Peggy's open mouth her gums are turning pink! That means her blood is moving again.

Stephen feels a new burst of energy. He ignores his shaky arms and keeps trying to restart Peggy's heart. When the oxygen runs out, his partner opens a second bottle.

More time passes. The crowd falls silent. Everyone is rooting for Peggy.

Finally, Stephen sees the puppy's chest rise. She is breathing on her own!

He stops pumping Peggy's heart and pulls the tube out of her throat. He holds the tube so that oxygen blows over the dog's face. Then he watches . . . and waits.

Mr. and Mrs. Shaw arrive home to see thick, black smoke billowing out of their house.

"It's unreal!" Mr. Shaw says. Two fire trucks and a police car are parked out front. Firefighters wearing bright yellow helmets and yellow-striped, gold uniforms swarm over their lawn. They are rolling up flat fire hoses. Groups of neighbors are walking around staring and talking.

A fireman shows Mr. Shaw the busted door and takes him through the house. Mrs. Shaw barely notices the damage. She runs from person to person asking, "Our dog? What about our dog?"

Much later Curtis learns what happened. By then his tired father is asleep on Nana's couch. His mother is driving him and Daniel to a neighbor's house to sleep. "Why are we going there?" Curtis asks. "Why don't we just go home?"

As gently as she can, Mrs. Shaw explains that Peggy accidentally started a fire. She tells them their house has been badly damaged and needs to be repaired.

She tells them Peggy is alive but at the vet.

Curtis shakes his head. "I don't believe you, Mommy." Deep inside he fears he can never go home again. And he is scared for Peggy. Maybe she has already died and his mom hasn't told him. Or, almost as bad, maybe everybody is mad at her.

Peggy did a bad thing. She started a fire that ruined his family's couch, TV, and video game player. Curtis worries. *If naughty Peggy is okay, will Daddy send her away? If he does, what will I do without her?*

Two days after the fire, Mrs. Shaw takes Curtis to visit their home. Together they wander about inside. Since black dust covers the windows, they use a flashlight to see. Curtis gasps at the ruined walls and melted refrigerator door. He looks up at the hole the firemen chopped in the kitchen ceiling and down at the chunks of ceiling lying at his feet. Everything stinks of smoke and burnt plastic. Curtis chokes on the smell and holds his nose. But even with his nose plugged, a bad taste fills his mouth.

For six long weeks, Mrs. Shaw and the boys live at friends' houses. Mr. Shaw stays at Nana's. He drives a truck during the day and works on the house until late every night. When Peggy leaves the vet, she stays with him. The vet warns Mr. Shaw to wake up often and poke the dog during the night to make sure she keeps breathing. Mr. Shaw does exactly that—no matter how tired he feels.

The next morning Mr. Shaw finds a

big, black stain on Nana's white carpet. The stain is right beside Peggy's open mouth. It comes from her breathing out the smoke that still clogs her lungs.

Ever so slowly things begin to get better. Mr. Shaw finishes his work on the house and buys a new television. It is not as big as the one that burned, but it works fine. The family finally moves back home, and Peggy begins to act like herself again. The family is happy. It hasn't been the same without her silly stunts.

One day Curtis takes Peggy outside to play in the yard. He throws a soccer ball for her to chase. To his delight she runs after it like she used to before the fire. Peggy grabs the ball with her mouth.

Then *POP!* Her sharp teeth poke a hole

in the ball and it goes flat.

Curtis freezes. He looks back at his watching parents. Will they be mad at Peggy for ruining his ball?

No. Mr. and Mrs. Shaw are smiling and laughing. "Don't worry," says Curtis's dad. "We will buy you another one."

Curtis smiles and hugs his best friend. The truth is, Peggy always means to be good. She just forgets sometimes. So whether she's been naughty or nice, one thing will never change. Everybody loves Peggy.

Get Out and Stay Out!

Never go back inside a burning building. These words of advice come from Sparky the spotted Dalmatian. Sparky is the official mascot of the National Fire Protection Association and for good reason. Dalmatians have lived in firehouses since horses pulled fire wagons. These canine long-distance runners raced alongside the team leading the way. Just as important, they kept the horses calm.

So listen to Sparky. He gives doggone good advice.

Super sneaky and stealthy, Olivia sets off on one of her nightly raids.

OLIVIA: THE CAT BURGLAR

Olivia might look like a sweet little kitty, but this sneaky cat leads a secret life of crime.

Chapter 1

Spring 2009, Milford, Connecticut

Olivia. Charged with more than 400 counts of robbery and holding on to stolen goods.

Also known as: Cow Kitty

Description: White with black spots, all-black ears, and black tail.

Scars and Marks: Beard-like black smudge under her chin.

Habits: A sneaky thief who goes to work when no one is looking, especially under cover of darkness.

Likes stuffed sharks and usually steals gloves in pairs.

Status: Last seen hiding out in Anne and Richard Weizel's backyard, in Milford, Connecticut. Warning! Suspect is unarmed and adorable.

Olivia, the little 8-pound (3.6 kg) kitty, leads a double life. During the day she plays the role of devoted house pet to the Weizels' sons—Josh, ten, and Jeremy, eight. But when the sun goes down, *beware!* This fluffy kitty turns into a sticky-footed thief. With one goal in mind, she scrambles over wooden fences and cuts through backyards. She prowls through the woods and prances across darkened streets. Every night she drags her loot home.

This feline crime spree begins when Anne Weizel convinces her husband, a newspaper reporter, that they should adopt a cat. To find one, Mrs. Weizel visits the "cat lady."

The cat lady takes in strays and finds them homes. Nearly twenty black, yellow, and tabby cats laze about her living room. They lie curled on the couch and stretched out on the floor. Fat cats and skinny cats. Old cats and baby cats.

The kitties rub against Mrs. Weizel's legs and make soft, rumbly, purring sounds. She pets first one, then another. It is so hard to choose. Finally, she scoops up a boy kitty and presses him against her cheek. "I want this one," she says.

Mrs. Weizel puts the kitten into a

plastic cat carrier as another scampers past. "That's his sister," the cat lady says.

Mrs. Weizel blinks. *Really?* The girl kitten immediately appeals to her. She loves its black and white coloring and dainty size. The little furry ball could fit inside a teacup. And the kitten's eyes! They're almond-shaped. Anne can't help herself. She takes both kittens.

At home, Josh and Jeremy squeal happily at the news of getting two kitties.

But Mr. Weizel looks into the cat carrier and sees four glowing eyes staring back. He groans. "You were supposed to get just one."

"Yes, but . . ." Mrs. Weizel tries to explain. She opens the carrier, and both kitties run for cover. The boy cat hides behind the couch. The girl cat scoots down to the cellar and disappears in a pile of boxes.

"We agreed on *one* cat only," Mr. Weizel says, throwing his hands in the air. "Please take the second one back."

Mrs. Weizel sighs. She wants both cats, but a deal is a deal. She will return the girl kitty as soon as she can catch her. Mrs. Weizel sets out some food. Overnight the food disappears, but the scared kitten remains out of sight.

Josh tries to get her to come out by dangling a string. Jeremy dishes up more food. "Here kitty, kitty . . ." Mrs. Weizel calls. Nothing works.

Two weeks pass.

The boy cat is getting used to his home. Mrs. Weizel puts him in the cellar hoping he can get his sister to come out. He does. When Mr. Weizel sees the girl kitten up close, he gives up. "She *is* kind of cute," he says. "I guess she can stay."

Mrs. Weizel names the boy Gabby and the girl Olivia. "Olivia fits," Mrs. Weizel says, "because she is so dainty and sweet. She looks like she should be taking piano lessons and attending school in France."

Once Olivia decides to join the family, she joins it in a big way. The little kitty with the big heart does not play favorites. She snuggles with everyone. She seems especially determined to win over Mr. Weizel. The dog-loving man of the house usually tries to avoid cats, but Olivia refuses to be ignored. She hops into Mr. Weizel's lap when he reads the newspaper. She winds around his legs when he stands in the kitchen. She curls up on his feet when he lies down.

Before long, Olivia rules all the animals in the house. That includes her big brother and two shy, droopy-eared beagles. Every day, Mrs. Weizel takes the dogs for a mile-long walk. Olivia not only insists on joining them. She leads the way, except when she sees a dog she doesn't know. Then Olivia darts behind a bush until the dog passes.

One freezing winter morning, knee-high snow is piled along the sidewalk. Mrs. Weizel and the dogs barely get started out the door before Olivia spots them leaving. Immediately the cat scoots in front of them. Holding her tail up high, she walks along like she is the boss of the world.

Every time the dogs stop to sniff or pee, Olivia stands and waits. When the beagles start walking, so does she. One dog dares to try moving ahead. *Yelp!* Olivia swats him. The beagle tucks his tail between his legs and slinks to the end of the line.

Neighbors notice Olivia leading the way. All along the street, they leave their breakfasts and hurry to their windows to watch the show. No one guesses that the leader of this strange parade has a secret —she is a cat burglar.

The Secret Life of Cats

What do cats do all day when they're home alone? Sleep? That's what most people think. But scientist Jill Villarreal wanted the real scoop. She gave "cat cams" to fifty house cats. The cat cams hung from their collars and snapped a photo every 15 minutes. Jill then studied the best 777 pictures. Guess what? When the family's away, the cat will play. Or watch TV. Or hang out with the dog. To Jill's surprise, kitties home alone take very few cat naps. Mostly they peer out windows! Maybe they're watching for you to come home.

Olivia sniffs a large pile of her "loot."

Chapter 2

STOP, THIEF!

Mrs. Weizel returns home from work one day and hears meowing coming from under her bed. She kneels down to look and finds Olivia and four tiny kittens. When the kittens are old enough, Mrs. Weizel gives three of them away. She keeps one. He grows bigger than his mother, but Olivia is still the boss.

Still nobody suspects her of doing anything wrong. Not even when Mrs. Weizel finds a gardening glove dropped on her front porch.

Hmm, she thinks. *A neighbor must have found it and thought it belonged to us.* The next day, another glove appears. Then another, and another. Every day for three months, Mrs. Weizel discovers a new glove lying on the steps. Every day she picks it up and tosses it in the washing machine with the rest of the laundry. She puts all the gloves in a large plastic garbage bag. *But who is leaving them?* Little did she know, the answer was right under her feet.

One day Jeremy and a friend are outside playing when Olivia appears carrying something in her mouth.

She drops the package in the grass, and Jeremy rushes over and picks it up. It is surprisingly heavy.

Jeremy runs inside and shows his mom. "Look what Olivia dragged home!" He unrolls a strip of cloth pockets holding a mini wrench, screwdrivers, and other tools.

Mrs. Weizel barely looks at the mini tool kit. She has other things on her mind.

Not wanting to be bothered with silly cat stories, Mrs. Weizel shoos Jeremy away. She is thinking about her mother, who has been very sick.

Later that evening, Mrs. Weizel happens to look out the window and spots Olivia crossing the street. The cat waddles slightly as she walks and keeps her front legs wide apart. Mrs. Weizel squints and leans forward. "Well, I'll be!" A stolen garden glove dangles from Olivia's mouth!

So Olivia is bringing the gloves home. But why?

Mrs. Weizel stops worrying to think. How far does Olivia roam to find all these gloves? Does she mistake gloves for birds, squirrels, or some other animal? Does she think they are cat toys? Or is she stealing because she misses her kittens? Maybe Olivia simply enjoys collecting gloves, like some humans collect stamps or rare coins. Mrs. Weizel adds this glove to the dozens of others in her garbage bag. What a strange habit. Mrs. Weizel continues to think it over.

Did You Know?

A group of cats is called a clowder.

One evening Olivia sits beside her food dish washing her face. Mrs. Weizel comes into the kitchen. She does not pet or even notice the cat. She just flops down at the kitchen table across from her husband. In her mother's house, a vase of freshly cut roses would be sitting on the table, but not here. Mrs. Weizel's table is covered with bills. Her husband will pay the most important ones. Others will have to wait.

Mr. Weizel looks up from the piles of paper. "What's wrong?" he asks.

"It's my mother," Mrs. Weizel says. "The doctor is starting her on treatments." After a pause, she adds, "Another bill collector called today."

Josh hears his parents talking and fears an argument is beginning. His parents fight a lot lately, and it scares Josh to hear them. Their angry words make his stomach hurt. Today he escapes by running upstairs to his room and lying down on his bed. Olivia must sense that he is upset. She goes upstairs with him and snuggles beside him. Josh pets her. The warm feel of her furry little body against his fingers makes him feel better.

Right now Olivia acts like she doesn't have a care in the world. She licks her paw and rubs it over her face. Then she stretches and purrs. But the kitty must be thinking something, because that night she suddenly changes her routine. Forget the gardening gloves, Olivia is sick of those. She is after bigger loot.

Why Do Cats Steal?

Scientists disagree. Some believe that "cat burglars" are not so much stealing as they are collecting. They think some kitties like certain things and can't help but add them to their stash. For these cats, it may be all about the hunt.

Other scientists think bringing home socks and toys is simply normal cat behavior. Stray cats drag home food to feed their kittens. Tame ones often bring their owners dead birds or mice. Cat burglars just get carried away—maybe because they like the attention.

She brings home a Winnie-the-Pooh purse, some rubber bands, and a yellow sponge.

A few days later, the loot gets even bigger. A stuffed shark with googly eyes, a matching pair of socks, sunglasses, and an oven mitt. Olivia begins showing great pride in her collection. She no longer drops them on the front porch and leaves. Instead, she sits beside them and meows— loudly, until someone comes to see what she's brought. "She doesn't stop until I open the door, pick her up, and kiss her," Mrs. Weizel says. Even if it is one o'clock in the morning, which it often is."

As the seasons change, the loot gets larger and larger. That spring Olivia finds a dust mop. Summer brings swim goggles and a beach ball. Running shoes turn up in the fall. Earmuffs, mittens, and a hand-knit Christmas tree ornament arrive in winter.

Meanwhile the family grows shorter of money. The bills keep piling up, and there's no money to pay them.

One day Mrs. Weizel steps outside to find a lady's big, black bra stretched across her front walk. She bursts into laughter. Then she carries the bra inside and waves it in front of Olivia's face. "You naughty kitty. Did you steal this?"

But Olivia is one cool cat. She shows no guilt. She just lies on her side blinking her almond-shaped eyes and twitching her soft, fluffy tail. Mrs. Weizel pets Olivia's long outstretched back. She could never resist that cuddly kitty.

The Weizels set up a "lost and found" box so neighbors can come get their stolen belongings.

Chapter 3

"STOLEN" TREASURE

Mrs. Weizel makes her friends laugh with stories of Olivia's thefts. Even better, it cheers up her mother. One Sunday Mrs. Weizel even stands up in church and admits that her sweet-looking pussycat is really a furry thief.

Word gets around about the four-legged burglar living on Ard Court. Neighbors who are missing things come by and paw through a "lost and found" box of Olivia's loot. One man makes repeated trips to take back a pair of expensive leather work gloves. He leaves them outside on the patio table because they get so dirty. He tries to ruin Olivia's plan by piling tools on top of them. But two can play at that game. The crooked feline his kids call "Cow Kitty" simply tugs the gloves out from underneath.

Meanwhile, the family's troubles go from bad to worse. Mr. Weizel loses his newspaper job and Mrs. Weizel's mother passes away. Every family member feels sad and upset.

Mrs. Weizel worries more than ever. She earns some money as a substitute teacher, but it is not enough. With her husband out of work, how will they pay for doctor appointments? For food? For clothing?

Mr. Weizel looks for a new job. At home he reads help-wanted ads on the Internet. Then he goes to the library to find more ads in the newspapers. Every day he calls reporters that he knows, people he used to work with. "Have you heard of any jobs?" he asks. They always answer, "No."

One day Mr. Weizel checks on a job near where he used to work. No luck. His shoulders slump as he climbs back into his car to drive home. He only drives a few blocks before his car sputters to a stop. Mr. Weizel looks at the dashboard of his car. Its gas pump symbol glows yellow.

"Oh, no!" Mr. Weizel grits his teeth and bangs his fist on the steering wheel.

So much is going wrong. First he gets behind on his bills. Then he loses his job. Now he runs out of gas. He doesn't know how this day could get any worse, or any better for that matter.

Mr. Weizel looks sad when he finally walks into the house. But he can't stay that way—not when his wife shows him two soggy rolls of toilet paper that Olivia had dragged home in the rain. "She delivered these at 2 a.m. And she looked so proud," says Mrs. Weizel. Mr. Weizel took the soggy rolls in his hand. Husband and wife cried with

> **Did You Know?**
>
> Cats have great night vision. In the dark they can see about six times better than humans.

laughter. It was the first time they felt happy in a while.

Like a faithful mail carrier, neither rain nor snow keeps Olivia from her rounds. Mr. Weizel admired her for always going out and getting the job done . . . even though she was stealing.

"You never give up, do you?" he asks the cat. "You just keep on trucking, going out every day and finding us stuff."

Mr. Weizel perks up. He makes a decision right then. He would work as hard at finding a job as Olivia does searching for presents. Every morning he wakes up curious to see what Olivia has brought.

His new attitude helps. Several months later he receives an email from an online newspaper. Would he like to work for them?

"I sure would!" Mr. Weizel writes back. The next day he packs up his camera and computer. On the way out the door he steps over a child's green flip-flop that Olivia had left on the step. Then off he goes with a smile on his face.

The whole family cheers up to see Dad back at work. Even Olivia seems happy. Her stealing continues for a while, but she no longer drags home two or three items a night. Some nights she doesn't bring anything home. Olivia stops bringing home gardening gloves completely until one night . . .

Mrs. Weizel is having a terrible day. Her car won't start, and she gets to work late. Once she arrives the kids she is teaching won't do their work. When she gets home, her own kids argue and complain. Most of all, Mrs. Weizel misses her mother. She wishes she had some of her mother's sweet-smelling rose bushes growing in her own yard. Just looking at them would boost her spirits.

Olivia climbs into her lap. Mrs. Weizel strokes her silky, soft fur and tries not to cry.

That night Olivia goes back on the job. A year had passed since she last brought home a gardening glove. And it had been several days since she brought home anything. But now the cuddly kitty sets off on one more hunt.

The sun is up before Mrs. Weizel hears Olivia's familiar meow. It's the tone that says, "Come look what I found for you."

Mrs. Weizel opens the front door and finds Olivia bearing a muddy glove.

"Thank you, Olivia," Mrs. Weizel says. She grasps one finger of the filthy glove and carries it to the washing machine. She throws it in. It swishes around with the rest of the load. Later, Mrs. Weizel removes the spanking clean glove and gasps in surprise.

It is off-white, cotton, and decorated with . . . red roses! Her mother's favorite!

Mrs. Weizel picks up Olivia and hugs her. She pins the glove to her bulletin board. "It comforts me to look at it," she says.

Olivia hardly ever hunts anymore. But what if she returns to a life of crime? What should the Weizels do then?

Doctor Cat

Feeling sad or afraid? Get a cat. You don't even have to pet it. Research shows that just having one around will calm you.

Dennis Turner is an animal behaviorist at Switzerland's University of Zurich. He says, "The fantastic thing about the cat is that it doesn't force itself on the person." A cat is there when you need it, but understands when you want to be alone.

Cats comfort depressed people. They help them make friends. And they lower their blood pressure. What could be more purr-fect?

They could sentence her to community service. A cat burglar in California rode in a parade to help the humane society raise money.

They could keep Olivia in the house if they wanted to put an end to her career once and for all.

But rather than get mad at their kitty for her strange behavior, the Weizels love her for it. Even when she brings home toilet paper. To them, it's not the gift. It's the thought that counts.

THE END

INDEX

Boldface indicates illustrations.

MORE INFORMATION

To find more information about the animal species featured in this book, check out these books and websites:

Face to Face With Orangutans,
National Geographic, 2011

Cats vs. Dogs,
National Geographic, 2009

National Geographic Kids "Creature Features: Orangutans"
kids.nationalgeographic.com/kids/animals/creaturefeature/
orangutan

Orangutan Foundation International
www.orangutan.org

National Geographic "Animals: Domestic Cat"
animals.nationalgeographic.com/animals/mammals/domestic-cat

National Geographic Kids "Games: Brainteasers Cool Cats"
kids.nationalgeographic.com/kids/games/puzzlesquizzes/
brainteasercoolcat

National Geographic Kids "Photos:
Dogs With Jobs"
kids.nationalgeographic.com/
kids/photos/dogs-with-jobs

National Geographic
"Animals: Domestic Dog"
animals.nationalgeographic
.com/animals/mammals/
domestic-dog

This book is dedicated to my own partner in crime, my husband, Neil.
—Aline Alexander Newman

CREDITS

Title page, Konrad Wothe/SuperStock; 4-5, Dr. Lee G. Simmons, Omaha's Henry Doorly Zoo; 6, Life on White/Alamy; 6 (BACK), Elenathewise/Dreamstime; 13, Lisa Turay/iStock-photo.com; 16, Omaha World-Herald; 25, David Allen Brandt/Getty Images; 25, Sonica83/Dreamstime; 26, Frans Lanting/National Geographic Stock; 34, Konrad Wothe/SuperStock; 36, Lorraine Shaw; 38, Lorraine Shaw; 47, Cynoclub/Dreamstime; 48, North News & Pictures Ltd.; 57, Gvictoria/Dreamstime; 58, North News & Pictures Ltd.; 67, Minden/SuperStock; 68, Autumn Driscoll; 70, Autumn Driscoll; 79, 0007filip/Dreamstime; 80, Autumn Driscoll; 89, Tzooka/Dreamstime; 90, Autumn Driscoll; 99, Atm2003/Dreamstime; 102, Life on White/Alamy ; 102 (Background), © Elena Elisseeva | Dreamstime

ACKNOWLEDGMENTS

A special thanks to:

Tracey Marshall and Stephen Buglass, for their invaluable detective work.

Amy and Steve Stevens, for adding to cat burglar lore.

Hope Irvin Marston, Jean Capron, Judy Ann Grant, Jeanne Converse, and Jule Lattimer, for critiquing my first draft.

Lee G. Simmons, DVM, for unearthing his photos of Fu Manchu.

Geza Teleki, for wise advice and moral support.

Regina Brooks, for handling the business end.

The National Geographic staff, especially Catherine Hughes, for recommending me to the Book Division, and Becky Baines, for never giving up on Fu Manchu.

I am grateful to the following experts:

Bonnie Beaver, DVM, Texas A&M University College of Veterinary Medicine

PD Dr. sc. Dennis C. Turner, Owner and Director of I.E.T./I.E.A.P., Hirzel, Switzerland

Suzanne Hetts, Ph.D., Animal Behavior Associates, Inc., Littleton, CO

Lori Perkins, Chairperson of AZA Orangutan Species Survival Plan and Director of Animal Programs at Zoo Atlanta

Above all, I thank the animal-loving families, brave firemen, and devoted zoo personnel for graciously sharing their stories with me. They made this project possible.

Book 3

ANIMAL SUPERSTARS!

And More True Stories of Amazing Animal Talents

Aline Alexander Newman

Published by the National Geographic Society
John M. Fahey, *Chairman of the Board and Chief Executive Officer*
Timothy T. Kelly, *President*
Declan Moore, *Executive Vice President; President, Publishing and Digital Media*
Melina Gerosa Bellows, *Executive Vice President; Chief Creative Officer, Books, Kids, and Family*

Prepared by the Book Division
Hector Sierra, *Senior Vice President and General Manager*
Nancy Laties Feresten, *Senior Vice President, Kids Publishing and Media*
Jonathan Halling, *Design Director, Books and Children's Publishing*
Jay Sumner, *Director of Photography, Children's Publishing*
Jennifer Emmett, *Vice President, Editorial Director, Children's Books*
Eva Absher-Schantz, *Design Director, Kids Publishing and Media*
Carl Mehler, *Director of Maps*
R. Gary Colbert, *Production Director*
Jennifer A. Thornton, *Director of Managing Editorial*

Staff for This Book
Becky Baines, *Project Editor*
Lisa Jewell, *Illustrations Editor*
Eva Absher-Schantz, *Art Director*
Ruthie Thompson, *Designer*
Grace Hill, *Associate Managing Editor*
Joan Gossett, *Production Editor*
Marfé Ferguson Delano, *Release Editor*
Lewis R. Bassford, *Production Manager*
Susan Borke, *Legal and Business Affairs*
Kate Olesin, *Assistant Editor*
Kathryn Robbins, *Associate Designer*
Hillary Moloney, *Illustrations Assistant*

Manufacturing and Quality Management
Phillip L. Schlosser, *Senior Vice President*
Chris Brown, *Vice President, NG Book Manufacturing*
George Bounelis, *Vice President, Production Services*
Nicole Elliott, *Manager*
Rachel Faulise, *Manager*
Robert L. Barr, *Manager*

The National Geographic Society is one of the world's largest nonprofit scientific and educational organizations. Founded in 1888 to "increase and diffuse geographic knowledge," the Society's mission is to inspire people to care about the planet. It reaches more than 400 million people worldwide each month through its official journal, *National Geographic,* and other magazines; National Geographic Channel; television documentaries; music; radio; films; books; DVDs; maps; exhibitions; live events; school publishing programs; interactive media; and merchandise. National Geographic has funded more than 10,000 scientific research, conservation, and exploration projects and supports an education program promoting geographic literacy.

For more information, please visit www.nationalgeographic.com, call 1-800-NGS LINE (647-5463), or write to the following address:
National Geographic Society
1145 17th Street N.W.
Washington, D.C. 20036-4688 U.S.A.

Visit us online at www.nationalgeographic.com/books

For librarians and teachers: www.ngchildrensbooks.org

National Geographic supports K–12 educators with ELA Common Core Resources. Visit natgeoed.org/ commoncore for more information.

More for kids from National Geographic: kids.nationalgeographic.com

For information about special discounts for bulk purchases, please contact National Geographic Books Special Sales: ngspecsales@ngs.org

For rights or permissions inquiries, please contact National Geographic Books Subsidiary Rights: ngbookrights@ngs.org

Trade paperback
ISBN: 978-1-4263-1091-1
Reinforced library edition
ISBN: 978-1-4263-1092-8

Table of CONTENTS

OPEE: THE MOTOCROSS BIKER PUP

Opee and Mike Schelin go airborne! They both love to ride Mike's dirt bike.

Ready to ride, Opee pants with excitement. His helmet has a camera on top.

Chapter 1

April 2006, San Diego, California

Opee the Australian (sounds like AH-STRALE-YAN) shepherd cocks his head and listens. Has Mike entered the garage? The devoted dog jumps to his feet and runs toward the sound. Barking excitedly, he leaps onto the gas tank of Mike Schelin's dirt bike. Opee's pink tongue hangs out. His front paws rest on the handlebars.

Mike grins. He slips a helmet and goggles on the happy dog's head. He hops on the bike behind Opee and kicks the starter with his heel. Off they go across the California desert.

Mike is a professional motocross (sounds like MOE-TOE-CROSS) racer. And so is Opee! Motocross is a form of cross-country motorcycle racing. Racers ride special motocross bikes, also called dirt bikes. They race on rugged tracks that are closed to normal traffic.

Mike and Opee's story started when Mike Schelin was 35 years old. Things had not been going well for him lately and he was unhappy. *Cheer up!* he told himself. But he didn't know how. So he sat down with a pad and pencil.

He made a list of all the things that made him feel good.

Later Mike read what he wrote. *Hmm,* he thought, *dogs are first on my list. I need a job that lets me bring a dog to work.*

Soon Mike quit his job selling computers and moved to San Diego, California. He met a man there who let Mike live in an old house for free. In return, Mike agreed to fix up the place. But something was missing. Mike needed a dog to keep him company.

He called a woman who had an Australian shepherd puppy for sale. They agreed to meet on a country road where 75 mailboxes stood in a row.

Mike spotted the mailboxes first. Then he saw a mother dog and puppy playing in the grass. The puppy had soft, floppy ears. His furry coat had patches of black, brown, and gray with white around his neck. His eyes were different colors. One was blue and the other was brown. Mike scooped him up, and slurp! The little furball stuck out his tongue and licked Mike's face. Mike paid the woman and drove home with the puppy.

Mike didn't think of the dog as a pet. He thought of him more as a friend, or even a brother. He named the pup Opee, his own nickname as a child.

The next day, Mike woke up to whining. "Are you hungry, fella?" Mike asked. He poured some kibble into a plastic bowl and fixed himself a cup of coffee.

The house was a mess. A table saw stood in the middle of the living room. Rows of bare wooden studs rose like jail bars at one end of the room. Piles of sweet-smelling sawdust littered the floor.

Mike grabbed a hammer and started to work. Opee followed behind, leaving paw prints in the dust. Later he curled up in Mike's toolbox to sleep.

One day, Mike and Opee drove to the hardware store for supplies. When they got there, Mike set the puppy on a flatbed cart. "Stay," he said. Opee did. Mike was surprised by how well he obeyed. "He just seemed to get it," Mike said.

On weekends, Mike relaxed by riding his dirt bike in the desert. He took Opee with him. Mike thought Opee would enjoy running off-leash. Maybe he'd run after lizards and snakes. But Opee chased Mike instead. He chased him uphill and downhill. Over bumps and pits and in clouds of dust. The dog never stopped.

Mike decided to buy a quad—a four-wheeled off-road motorbike with a seat big enough for two. Now Opee could ride along! But how to keep the dust out of Opee's eyes? Mike had an idea. First he cut a slit in the middle of a sock. Then he slipped a pair of goggles through the slit and tied the ends of the sock under Opee's chin. Perfect! Opee jumped onto the seat and off they went.

Motorbikes are loud. Other dogs might have hated the noise. They might have jumped off the seat in fear. Not Opee.

One Sunday Mike didn't go to the desert. Instead, he wanted to ride his street bike to Santa Barbara, another city in California. His street bike is a big, rumbling Harley-Davidson motorcycle. Mike hadn't ridden the Harley in a while. So he took it for a test-drive around the block.

"Opee was at the gate going crazy," Mike said. "He was barking and jumping." The minute Mike let his dog loose, Opee surprised him by jumping up on the gas tank. "Okay," Mike said, hugging his dog. "I'll take you for a spin."

Mike started slow. The dog didn't blink. Mike went faster. The dog stayed put. When the speed reached 50 miles an hour (81 km/h), Opee crouched down closer to the bike. When the road curved, Opee leaned into the turns. *This dog is a natural,* Mike thought.

Mike hurried home and dashed into the house. Grabbing his extra helmet, he sawed a chunk out of the back so it would fit around Opee's head. Then he put the helmet, goggles, and a backpack on the pup. They were about to leave when Mike had another thought. He found some rope and tied Opee to him, just in case the dog lost his balance.

To Santa Barbara and back is 300 miles (483 km)—a long trip on a motorcycle. Mike wondered how long Opee would last.

Surprise! Opee made it the entire way.

Feeling Upset?

Get a pup.

Dogs understand when people are nervous or scared. Seeing you cry makes a dog feel bad. It will tuck its tail and bow its head, say scientists at the University of London, in England. A dog will snuggle against you and give you a doggie hug. You can bury your face in its soft fur, and it will lick your cheek.

Pretty soon, you will stop thinking about yourself and think about your pup instead. You might even smile.

Mike and his loyal
canine partner
look sharp riding
the hills.

Chapter 2

UPPING the STAKES

The next weekend, Mike and Opee returned to the desert. This time Opee walked right past the quad and jumped on Mike's dirt bike. Riding a dirt bike is harder than riding a motorcycle or quad. Keeping balance over bumps is difficult and tiring. Mike decided to take Opee for a test spin. No problem! Soon they were riding longer and faster than Mike's motocross pals.

Other riders urged Mike to enter the Lake Elsinore Grand Prix (sounds like PREE) with Opee. Forty years ago, a popular movie was made about this 100-mile (161-km) motocross race. Today nearly 1,000 people compete in it.

But riding for fun in the desert is one thing. Competitive racing is quite another. "They won't let a dog in that race," Mike said.

"Sure they will," insisted his friends. "They let someone else do it once."

Mike agreed to give it a try. The first thing he did was take Opee shopping. Nobody sold motocross gear for dogs. But Mike bought Opee the best-fitting helmet, goggles, and padded jersey he could find.

On a chilly November morning, Mike and Opee drove to Lake Elsinore, California. They reported to the check-in table. Mike paid the race fee and signed them up. He picked up two wristbands and three white signs with his number on them. He carefully attached the signs to his dirt bike. He slipped on one wristband and slid the other onto Opee's front leg.

Mike checked his gas and warmed up his engine. Opee hopped on and Mike drove slowly toward the raceway. The crowd separated to let them through the gate.

Mike gasped at the dazzling sight of row upon row of helmeted riders dressed in padded suits. Every rider sat on a brightly colored dirt bike with bumpy tires. It looked like a lineup from a parade. To be safe, Mike and Opee took a place in the back. The race can get rough. Accidents happen. Mike didn't want to put Opee at risk.

A woman carrying a clipboard walked up and down the lines. She inspected each bike and rider. Were they registered? Were they wearing the proper gear? When the woman reached Mike and Opee, she smiled. Still smiling, she went down her list. Check. Check. Mike and Opee passed inspection.

As everyone waited for the race to begin, some of the riders bounced on their seats. Others talked or laughed nervously. Mike squeezed and released his hand brakes. Opee sat patiently and barely moved.

Finally, a man yelled through a bullhorn. The race was starting! Another man standing on a platform waved a green flag. The first row of riders roared away. Each one left a burst of smoke behind. The flag waved again and again. Row after row of racers sped off. Mike and Opee's row was coming up soon. Mike leaned forward and shifted his weight.

The flag came down. They were off!

The uphill track immediately changed to dirt. Mike saw hay bales and a string of colored flags ahead. It was a corner. He and Opee leaned into it. Mike slowed and stuck his leg out for balance. A rider ahead of them went too fast. His bike crashed in the dirt. Mike jerked the handlebars and swerved around him.

The entire route was closed to traffic. Only racers could use it today. But the raceway kept changing. First it was dirt.

Then it was pavement. Then dirt again. It went uphill and down. It twisted and turned. For a while it wound right through the center of town.

Clusters of men and women stood on the grass bordering the route. Little kids in baseball caps perched on their fathers' shoulders. Everyone turned toward the roar of the bikes. As the riders whizzed by, the people cheered. "Hey, look!" someone yelled. "There's a dog in the race!"

People waved and shouted. The cheering grew louder when Mike and Opee rode by. Mike had never heard anything like it. He felt like a rock star.

Race officials stood at checkpoints along the way. They waved yellow flags to warn riders of turns and intersections.

Doggie Daredevils

Motocross is dangerous. People can get hurt or killed. That's why motocross is called an "extreme sport." Besides competing against others, extreme sport athletes also battle nature. They may face fierce winds, giant waves, snow, ice, finger-numbing cold, or blistering heat. Contestants need both physical and mental strength.

Dogs take part in extreme sports, too. The best known event is the Iditarod (sounds like EYE-DIT-ur-odd). Held in Alaska, it's an 1,100-mile (1,770-km) race for sled dogs. The winners of that truly are "top dogs."

Crashes happened anyway. Rescue vehicles patrolled the track. They towed trailers to pick up broken bikes and bring them back. Ambulances stood by to help.

The race was a test of skill. It was more about staying power than speed. "We're not in it to win," Mike told himself. "We just want to finish." Even so, he and Opee passed 100 riders along the way.

Mike and Opee made it to the checkered flag at the finish line and sputtered to a stop. Mike yanked off their helmets and threw an arm around his partner. "Good dog, Opee," he said and kissed his pal's wet, black nose. "Good dog!"

This dog is special, Mike thought. *This dog can make a difference.* Right then and there Mike set a new goal. He would use

Opee to help people. He would take him
to hospitals to visit sick kids. He would
register him as a therapy dog. But first
Mike wanted Opee to do something no
other dog had ever done. He decided to
enter them in the most challenging
motocross race of all—the Baja (sounds
like BA-HA) 500 in Mexico.

The Baja 500 was expensive. Race fees
alone were almost a thousand dollars.
Then there was food, hotels, and gasoline
to pay for. Mike knew he couldn't afford it
on his own. He needed a sponsor. Sponsors
are people or companies who help pay an
athlete's expenses. In return, the athlete
wears clothes and uses equipment that
advertises the sponsor's name. But how
would Mike ever find such a deal?

Mud is no match for Mike and Opee, who love to get dirty on the course.

Chapter 3

Lucky for Mike and Opee, they had already met the person who would become their sponsor. It happened at the Lake Elsinore motocross race. As Mike and Opee zipped around the track that day, all of a sudden...*CLANK!* Mike looked over his shoulder and saw his muffler lying in the dirt! He pulled off to the side and skidded to a stop. "Stay," he told Opee.

Mike ran and picked up the muffler. The metal was so hot it melted his leather gloves. "Ouch!" Mike dropped the muffler and stood there feeling defeated. Without the muffler, the noise of his engine would be deafening.

A stranger came to the rescue. He threw a bucket of water on the muffler to cool it. Someone else handed Mike a shoelace. Mike used it to tie the muffler to his bike. Then he and Opee got back into the race and finished it.

Afterward Mike met the stranger who had helped him. His name was Marty Mooks, and he was a former motocross racer. Marty fell in love with Opee. He decided he wanted to help Opee and Mike race together. Marty gave Mike a new muffler and helped him get sponsors. These sponsors gave Mike free dog food, racing equipment, and money to help him compete.

The Baja 500 was a very different race from Lake Elsinore. At Lake Elsinore racers drove around and around the same track. At Baja they never covered the same ground twice. At nearly 500 miles (805 km), the Baja was also five times longer. Racers needed a cell phone in case they got lost. They also needed a chase vehicle to carry food and water for them. And unlike Lake Elsinore, Baja had a time limit. Racers had to finish within 18 hours.

But the biggest difference was that not only dirt bikes competed at Baja. People also raced four-wheeled bikes called ATVs, stripped-down automobiles with special tires, street motorcycles, cars, and trucks. Some of the trucks were as big and powerful as monster trucks.

Baja was scary. Riders had to pay attention every second. Mike decided that he and Opee couldn't do it alone. They would race as a team. Three of Mike's friends offered to help: a teenage boy, an army sergeant (sounds like SAR-JENT), and another motocross racer. They would run the race in relays. Everyone would take a turn on the dirt bike. But Opee and Mike would ride the longest.

The five-member team traveled to Mexico in Mike's old van. Once there, the men packed the van with supplies and prepared Mike's bike. They changed the oil and tuned up the engine. They checked the tires and brakes. They tested the lights. They made sure everything ran perfectly. Nobody wanted a breakdown in the desert.

Mike worked with Opee. He had been teaching him voice commands. Now they practiced again. "Set it up," Mike said, when they came to a jump. The dog instantly dropped down so Mike could see over his head.

> **Did You Know?**
>
> In some places, Australian shepherds are used to herd sheep and cattle.

At the bottom of a steep, sandy hill, Mike stopped the bike. He knew the bike could flip over backward as it climbed up. "Get off," he told Opee. Opee leaped to the ground. Mike gunned the engine and roared toward the top. Opee ran and got there first.

Mike stopped, the dog jumped back on, and off they went. Mike smiled. *We're ready,* he thought.

On race day, Opee looked like a pro. He wore a special doggie helmet with a camera on it. He also wore padding around his neck and a high-tech, inflatable chest protector. The human members of his team also wore special protective gear.

It was a good thing they did, too. The Baja was wilder than the craziest roller coaster ride. It had uphills, downhills, rocks, sand pits, mud holes, dust, and deep ditches. Mike's teenage friend only lasted 28 miles (45 km). The sergeant gave up after 60 (97 km). The other motocross racer made it 150 (241 km). But Mike and Opee? They just kept going, mile after mile, hour after hour.

Just before dark, Mike and Opee were riding fast. Mike wanted to reach the beach before the sun went down. He squeezed the gas. The speedometer spun. And then it happened. They were zooming along at an amazing 75 miles an hour (121 km/h) when they hit a silt bed. "A silt bed is like riding through flour," said Mike. "It will swallow your bike."

The back end of the bike spun out. It crashed to the ground. Both Mike and Opee flew through the air. Mike landed on his face in the dirt with his arms straight out in front of him. `Opee rolled to a stop near him.

Groaning, Mike climbed to his knees and crawled to his dog. He checked him for injuries. Opee had a scrape on his nose and another on his paw. Nothing serious, thank goodness. Mike sighed with relief.

Only then did he notice the blood. It was running into his boot from a cut on his calf.

It was decision time. Should they continue or drop out now? Mike was still thinking when Opee decided for him. The determined dog jumped back on the bike.

That day Mike and Opee rode for over 200 teeth-rattling miles (322 km). They reached the finish line with ten minutes to spare. Opee became the first dog ever to complete the Baja 500!

"It was the hardest thing I've done in my life," Mike said. "And I couldn't have done it without my dog."

Opee just wagged his tail.

Emergency!

Suppose your dog got hurt. Having a doggie first-aid kit would help. Here are some things to put in it. Make sure to have an adult help you if your pet really does get hurt.

1. Phone numbers for your local vet, an emergency vet clinic, and a poison control center
2. A list of your dog's medicines and shots
3. A muzzle or strips of cloth for tying the dog's mouth shut. (A hurt animal might bite.)
4. Nonstick bandages
5. Medical tape
6. Cornstarch to put on bleeding toenails
7. Blanket or towels

Sidewinder, a.k.a. Dunkirk Dave, is a small, female groundhog. She was found in this basket.

SIDEWINDER: GROUNDHOG WEATHER WONDER

Like this one, most groundhogs are brown and gray. But some are black or even white.

Chapter 1

April 2005, Dunkirk, New York

A wounded baby groundhog trembled in fear. Someone had wrapped her in a blanket and put her in a basket. Just hours before, she and her brothers and sisters were probably eating dandelions in a grassy field. Now her siblings were gone. Her mother was nowhere to be seen. The terrified baby was all alone.

Meanwhile, Bob Will was driving home from visiting his parents. The setting sun glowed red over Lake Erie as he pulled into his driveway.

Bob got out of his jeep and walked around to the front of his house. He saw a beat-up wicker basket propped against his screen door. "What's this?" he wondered as he peeked inside.

Did You Know?

In the spring, female groundhogs give birth to two to six newborns.

"Oh, no!" Another hurt animal!

Bob is a wildlife rehabilitator (sounds like REE-UH-BILL-UH-TAY-TER). A wildlife rehabilitator is a person who has been trained to help wild animals in need. Sometimes people dropped off hurt animals at Bob's house. Once it was a swan with a broken wing. Another time a blind turtle turned up on his front steps. But this little baby groundhog tore at Bob's heart. She reminded him of the very first groundhog he had ever saved.

Bob was ten years old then. He found an injured groundhog in a farmer's field and took it home. Someone had shot it. "That's a throwaway animal!" a nosy neighbor said. "What are you taking care of that for?"

The unkind words made Bob want to cry. "Every animal has a right to life," he said. "This groundhog did not deserve to be shot." At home, Bob taped bandages over the groundhog's wounds. He fed him sugar water with an eyedropper. The groundhog slowly got better. Months later, Bob released him back into the wild.

"That gave me a feeling of power," he said. "I had saved an animal's life."

Now it was fifty years later, and people were still shooting groundhogs because they dig holes and sometimes eat crops. Bob shook his head sadly and brought the basket inside. He set it down beside a tower of plastic animal carriers, called kennels (sounds like KEN-uls). Then he went through his bathroom medicine cabinet. As a wildlife rehabilitator, Bob kept that cabinet well stocked with medical supplies.

Bob was washing the groundhog when his roommate and helper, Bill Verge, arrived home. Bill saw blood in the bathwater. "What happened?" he asked.

"I found her on the doorstep," Bob said. "Somebody shot her."

Bill pitched in to help. He held the groundhog while Bob bandaged her head. The animal was so weak she couldn't open her eyes. Bill laid her on a towel and put her in a kennel. He packed hot water bottles around her to keep her warm.

That night Bob woke up every two hours to feed the baby groundhog. But during the day, he taught school. That's when Bill took over the feedings. Bill worked at home. He and Bob ran a side business repairing old typewriters. The money they earned from this business paid for animal food and supplies.

Between them, Bob and Bill cared for the baby groundhog around the clock. But the animal was so thin she looked like a sack of bones. When she lifted her head, it flopped.

Hungry, Hungry Groundhogs!

Groundhogs aren't called "hogs" for nothing. A single animal eats a pound (0.5 kg) of greens a day and can destroy a garden. To keep groundhogs out without harming them, try these tips:

1. Play a radio in the garden.
2. Ask an adult to put in lights and alarms.
3. Dig a ditch around the garden. Bury woven wire fencing in it one foot deep (0.3 m). This should leave about three feet (0.9 m) of fencing aboveground. Leave the top wobbly so groundhogs can't climb it.

All the little groundhog did was lie on her side with her feet pawing the air. Bob started calling her "the girl who can't walk." He decided to take her to the vet.

The vet set the tiny limp animal on his table. He parted her fur with his fingers and looked at her wound. He shone a light in her ears and gently pressed the bones in her legs. "Her wounds are clean," the vet said. "They are starting to heal."

Bob smiled.

But there was more to come. "The bullet has damaged her brain," the vet said. "I'm afraid she might not make it."

Bob's shoulders slumped. He scooped up his girl and went home. But he did not give up.

For two months straight Bob got up at night to squirt food into the groundhog's mouth. She ate a mixture of sweet potatoes and monkey biscuits that Bob ground up in a blender. Monkey biscuits are made of nuts and grain. They are rock-hard and good for a groundhog's teeth.

One day Bob laid his hand against the groundhog's belly. For the first time it felt round and plump. "Woo-hoo!" Bob whooped. "Our girl is going to make it!"

Now if only she could learn to walk.

Six months passed. One day Bob set "the girl who can't walk" on the floor with some other rescued groundhogs. At least she could hang out with her friends. But this little girl groundhog did more than that. She copied them and tried to stand up.

Bob watched as she pushed herself to her feet. He held his breath as she wobbled in place. And he groaned in disappointment when she toppled over.

Stand up. Fall down. Stand up. Fall down.

It went on like this for days. Bob could not believe how hard the little groundhog tried. She simply wouldn't give up.

Then one day she did it. The girl stayed standing!

A few days later she took a step. Then she took another and another. Bill chuckled as he watched her make up for lost time. "Our girl that can't walk," he joked, "is always on the run!"

There was just one problem. The damage she had suffered had jumbled the signals in her brain. The plucky little groundhog could only walk in circles.

Crunch!
Sidewinder nibbles
on lettuce. In the
wild, veggie-loving
groundhogs eat
plants and grasses.

Chapter 2

GROUNDHOG DAY!

Bob and Bill finally named the little groundhog. They called her "Sidewinder" because she couldn't walk straight. Bob looked at her sleeping in her kennel one night. He noticed that she held a corner of a towel in her mouth. *How come?* he wondered. Then he heard a soft sucking sound. "Bill, come here," Bob whispered.

Bill tiptoed over. He looked and listened. He heard it, too. The little groundhog was sucking on the towel. It was just like a baby sucking on a pacifier.

Now that Sidewinder could stand, she could eat on her own. And boy, was she hungry! She crunched carrots. She gobbled up lettuce. She snacked on corn on the cob. And she topped it all off with lemon cake for dessert.

The trouble was that mealtimes took forever. Wild groundhogs sit while they chow down. Not Sidewinder. She took one bite of food. Then she walked in a circle. She took a second bite. She looped around again. Round and round she went.

Sometimes she walked through her food. Carrots and biscuits scattered all about. Much of it ended up uneaten.

This worried Bill. All that walking used up a lot of energy. Sidewinder needed to eat more food than other groundhogs, not less.

Bob and Bill had an idea. When it was time to eat, they put Sidewinder and her food inside a large box. There she had to walk in smaller circles. Now she could finish a meal in three hours. It no longer took all day.

Bob was proud of Sidewinder. She had overcome so much. Maybe she would be up for a new challenge—Groundhog Day.

Groundhog Day comes on February 2. That's right in the middle of winter. People are often tired of winter by then. They are eager for spring. They like having an excuse for a celebration. You can guess what animal this celebration is about!

Bob and Bill were in charge of finding the groundhogs used in New York State. It started back in 1967. That year Bob brought a rescued groundhog to school. He showed it to his students.

The school custodian got really excited. He called the newspaper. "Have I got a story for you!" he said.

The paper sent a reporter to school. The reporter named the groundhog Dunkirk Dave, after their town. He asked Bob if the groundhog could

Did You Know?

Groundhogs dig holes called burrows. A burrow can be longer than a school bus.

forecast the weather. Maybe Dunkirk Dave could be New York's version of Punxsutawney (sounds like PUNKS-SUH-TAW-NEE) Phil!

Phil was another groundhog. He lived indoors in a town called Punxsutawney, Pennsylvania. Every Groundhog Day a group of men brought him outside to forecast the weather.

This was an old idea. It first came from Germany. People there held a festival called Candlemas (sounds like KAN-DUHL-MAS) on February 2. Part of this holiday was about the weather. It also had to do with a furry animal called a badger (sounds like BAJ-ER). If the sun was bright enough on Candlemas, a badger would see its shadow. Uh-oh! That meant winter would last another six weeks. But if the day was cloudy the badger would not see its shadow. That meant, "Hello, spring!"

When people came from Germany to the United States, they could not find any badgers. They did find groundhogs. In the 1800s, farmers in Pennsylvania began using them instead. On February 2 they watched to see if a groundhog saw its shadow. They had a picnic the same day.

Every year the picnic got bigger. Newspapers printed stories about it. More people wanted to know if the groundhog saw its shadow. More states began to celebrate Groundhog Day. In New York, Dunkirk Dave became the star of the show.

But groundhogs only live about 15 years. So, many have played the part.

Wild Weather Quiz

Today computers help us forecast the weather. Long ago people watched animals for signs that the weather was changing. Here are some of those signs. Do you know which ones are true?

1. Pigs gather sticks before a storm.
2. Crickets chirp faster as it gets warmer.
3. Frogs croak louder and more often just before it rains.
4. When ladybugs swarm, expect a day that is warm.

Answer: They are all true.

"It is important to have a groundhog that is calm around people," Bob says. A scared one might bite somebody.

Bob thought Sidewinder might be perfect for the role. To find out, he took her to meet his students.

In Bob's class, all of the kids had special needs. It set them apart. Sometimes they felt left out. But all that changed when Bob brought Sidewinder into class. Everyone wanted to watch her turn circles. They got in line to hold and pet her. Sidewinder seemed to love everybody.

"What soft fur you have," said one girl.

"What big teeth!" said a boy.

Their excitement spread. "What's going on in Mr. Will's room?" asked a boy passing by in the hall. He took a peek.

Suddenly lots of kids wanted to come into the room. Sidewinder made Bob's students feel important.

In one way, she and they were alike. She also had disabilities (sounds like DIS-UH-BILL-UH-TEES) that made it hard for her to learn. Bob explained how Sidewinder kept trying. She never gave up. Her story gave the kids hope. If they kept trying, maybe they could do things that were hard for them, too.

> **Did You Know?**
>
> When scared, groundhogs give a high whistle. That's why they're also called "whistle pigs."

At the end of the day Bob smiled to himself. Sidewinder did not get scared around strangers. She kept her cool. He thought she would make a great Dunkirk Dave come Groundhog Day.

On Groundhog Day, an antique dollhouse sets the stage for Sidewinder to play the role of Dunkirk Dave.

Chapter 3

A STAR IS BORN

Groundhog Day finally rolled around. At last it was Sidewinder's big day! Bob and Bill got up long before sunrise. Bill tended to the squirrels and other animals they cared for. He filled their water dishes and fed them. He changed their bedding and gave them medicine. Suddenly he heard a loud clanking noise. It was coming from Sidewinder's kennel.

"Sounds like Sidewinder wants some food," Bill said.

"She probably does," said Bob, laughing. "But today she will just have to wait. She will get plenty to eat once the sun comes up."

Sidewinder kept up the racket. She banged and banged the heavy hook holding her kennel door shut. *CLANK! CLANK! CLANK! Where's my dinner? CLANK! CLANK! CLANK!*

The hook was not a dinner bell. But Sidewinder thought it was. She had learned this trick all on her own. One day she banged that hook and food appeared. Aha! She banged the hook another time and it happened again. The men realized what she wanted and fed her. Then Sidewinder began banging the hook whenever she was hungry. And Bob and Bill were happy to help, except for today.

This was the one day of the year when Sidewinder must be patient. Today she would play the role of Dunkirk Dave. It was up to her to pop out of the groundhog hole in Bob's backyard. A crowd of people would be there. Everyone would be eager to find out if the groundhog saw her shadow.

The day before Groundhog Day, Bob worried about something. The weather had been warm that winter, and the snow had melted in Bob's backyard. The ground was bare. Wild animals were out looking for food. Bob had spotted a fox close by. He also had seen a skunk. Either one might come poking around his yard. That would put Sidewinder in danger. Foxes and skunks eat groundhogs! Bob thought for a while about how to keep Sidewinder safe.

Then he remembered his mother's old dollhouse. Her father made it for her when she was a little girl. Bob found the toy and carried it into the backyard. He paused for a minute before setting it down. His grandpa had built the dollhouse almost one hundred years ago. *It is a shame to do this,* Bob thought. *But Mom would understand.*

He took a saw and cut a hole through the bottom of the dollhouse. He made the hole as big around as the groundhog hole. Then he sat the house over the top.

And now it was almost show time! Bob carried Sidewinder outdoors. "Our guests will be here any minute," he told her.

It was still black as night when Bob opened the dollhouse roof and put Sidewinder inside. When he closed it she was nice and safe. Behind the house stood a miniature windmill. A sign hung on the tower. It read "Dunkirk Dave."

Then Bob went back indoors and changed into his best suit. He carefully tied his tie and combed his hair. The smell of coffee filled the air as he put doughnuts and cups on a table. For the children he had a special treat. He had bought furry, groundhog finger puppets for them. They felt soft and cuddly like Sidewinder.

Did You Know?

Sometimes groundhogs gobble up insects, snails, and birds' eggs.

Groovy Groundhogs

1. Groundhogs are rodents, like mice and beavers.
2. A groundhog's teeth never stop growing.
3. Groundhogs are also called "woodchucks" and "marmots."
4. Groundhogs spend most of their lives underground.
5. Groundhogs mostly sleep in winter.
6. Groundhogs can swim.
7. Foxes, skunks, and snakes often move into abandoned groundhog burrows.
8. Groundhogs can climb trees.
9. Groundhogs love to lie in the sun.

Every kid who came to visit would get a puppet. Bob hoped this day would encourage people to stop thinking of groundhogs as throwaway animals. He hoped it would help stop people from killing them.

Bob heard the rumble of a car engine. He peeked out his sliding glass doors. A white news van had just arrived. Bob saw photographers, reporters, college students, parents, and schoolchildren gathered in his yard. He went to join them. Everyone was waiting for the sun to come up.

When it did, Bob knelt beside the dollhouse. He set a paper plate of lettuce and lemon cake on the ground. He put a finger to his lips. "Shh," he said.

The crowd went quiet. Bob knocked on the side of the dollhouse. A small brown head appeared at the window. One tiny eye looked out.

Bob jiggled the plate. "Have some lemon cake," he said.

Groundhogs can hear sounds that people can't. Sidewinder listened carefully. If she heard anything scary she would not come out.

Everyone waited.

Sidewinder twitched her whiskers. She turned her head. Her body stretched out like a sausage. POP! Sidewinder slipped through the window and out of the dollhouse.

She nibbled at the lemon cake.

Bob looked at the cloudy sky. He looked at Sidewinder. He did not see a shadow. "We're going to have an early spring," he said. The crowd cheered.

The television crew packed up their stuff. A few people came forward to pet Sidewinder and chat with Bob. Eventually the crowd left.

Sidewinder was a big hit as Dunkirk Dave. Now she's a star! Hundreds of people have watched her videos online. Thousands more have seen her picture. A reporter in California heard about the disabled groundhog and the men who cared for her. She flew across the country to write about them. Other newspapers reprinted her story. Now Bob, Bill, and Dunkirk Dave are known from coast to coast.

Maybe Sidewinder did run in circles, but her message was straight as an arrow. "Look at me," her actions said. "We groundhogs are well worth saving."

These cool cats are ready to rock and roll! *MEEE-WOW!*

TUNA: KITTY ROCK STAR

Tuna looks ready to sing for her favorite treat. That's tuna fish, of course!

Chapter 1

Born to PURR-FORM

Spring 2003, Chicago, Illinois

A white kitten with big green eyes sat on a cardboard box. She looked very cute. Her name was Tuna. She had just been plopped down in a place she didn't know. Bright lights shone down from metal poles. They made her fur hot to the touch. A panting dog waited his turn in a corner. Tuna was having her picture taken.

"Most kittens would run," said Tuna's owner. Her name is Samantha Martin. Samantha loves cats. In fact, she loves all animals. She studied the care and raising of them in college. She dreamed of training animals for television and movies. When a photographer needed a kitten for a pet food ad, she offered her cat Tuna for the job. Now the photographer gripped a heavy camera and circled Tuna like a hungry wolf.

Samantha held her breath. *Please, Tuna,* she thought. *Don't bolt.*

The brave kitten stayed. She held her pose like a supermodel.

"Great!" the photographer said. "I got some good shots."

Samantha beamed. She opened a can of tuna fish, and the little kitty gobbled it up.

Before she got Tuna, Samantha trained rats. Her personal zoo also included a raccoon that could play basketball and a groundhog that could raise a flag. She had also trained a chicken, a duck, and a goose to play tiny musical instruments. But none of these acts drew a large enough audience for Samantha to earn a living from them.

To make it in show business, Samantha needed to train more popular animals. Watching Tuna in action started her thinking. Cat actors were much in demand. Somebody had to provide them. Why not Samantha?

"Tuna," Samantha said. "We're going to make you a star."

The next day Samantha brought out more tuna fish. She gave Tuna a nibble.

Then she waggled a long stick in front of her.

Tuna leaped and pounced, chasing the stick. The second Tuna's paw hit the stick, Samantha snapped a clicker. Then she gave the cat a bit of fish. They did this several times. Then, flash! Tuna realized that the click meant food. She had to touch the stick to get it.

The next day, Samantha brought out a push-button bell. Now she placed the stick on that. When Tuna touched the stick, she got nothing. She touched it again. Still nothing. Tuna scrunched her brow and twitched her tail. Maybe if she twirled around. *DING!* Tuna accidentally touched the bell. Samantha gave her a bit of fish. It took several lessons before Tuna figured out what Samantha wanted her to do.

Finally, Samantha gave Tuna a treat only if she actually rang the bell.

DING! CLICK. Treat!

Now Tuna knew her first trick.

The cat purred all through her training. *Hmm*, Samantha thought. *Tuna never used to purr. This must make her happy.* Most of the time Tuna was crabby. When Samantha picked her up, Tuna clawed to get down. If Samantha rubbed behind her ears, Tuna shook her head and walked away. But now Tuna came running when Samantha blew her training whistle. She quickly mastered trick after trick. "Tuna, you're brilliant," Samantha told her.

Did You Know?

Nearly a third of U.S. households own at least one cat.

But would Tuna perform for a crowd of people? There was one way to find out.

Samantha packed up Tuna's props. She wrote her name in glitter on the side of her pet carrier. Then she put Tuna inside and they left for California. They were going to a big fair where many pet lovers meet. Samantha could put Tuna's skills to the test there.

When they arrived at the fair, there were thousands of people strolling the grounds. Samantha lugged Tuna and her props through the crowd. She lugged them past a woolly poodle standing on a metal table. She lugged them past row upon row of big, heavy fish tanks. She lugged them past hamsters snoozing in metal cages. Samantha ignored them all. She needed to find the perfect spot for Tuna to perform.

Kitty "High Five"

You can train your cat to high-five. Ask your parents to buy a clicker and a bag of kitty treats at the pet store. Then sit on the floor with your cat. Hold the clicker in one hand. Grasp a treat between the fingers of your other hand. Now jiggle the treat in front of your cat. The second he swats for it, click and give him the treat. Do this over and over. Soon your kitty will slap you five whenever you click, even without a treat.

Aha! Samantha spied an empty countertop. She set Tuna's carrier down and called out to people walking past. "Hey!" she shouted. "Check out my cat. My cat needs a job."

A small crowd gathered. Samantha opened the pet carrier door and lured Tuna out with her favorite treat. The tricky kitty ignored all the people. She rang her bell. She rolled over. She jumped through a hoop. The crowd laughed and clapped, and Samantha grinned. What a cat! Tuna had what it takes. Maybe they would get lucky. Maybe Tuna would be discovered and become an actor.

Instead, a dog appeared.

Did You Know?

Like dogs, cats sweat through their paws.

Tuna froze. How dare this big mutt invade her space! Before Samantha could stop her, the cat leaped onto the dog's back. *EEEYOW!* She dug in her claws.

The dog whirled. Tuna screeched.

Fur flew as Samantha stood there in shock. Then as suddenly as everything started, it stopped. The fearless Tuna jumped back on the counter. Samantha stuffed her into her carrier and shut the door. The dog owner yanked his animal away.

After that Samantha put Tuna on a leash. She scheduled shows at libraries, schools, and birthday parties. These would not pay much. But at least Tuna would get some practice. Samantha prayed that their big break would come soon.

Head down, paws tucked in, Tuna soars over the hurdles.

Lights, Camera, ACTION!

Tuna loved performing, but it cost a lot of money to travel to shows. Samantha couldn't earn much at other jobs because Tuna took up almost all her time. Samantha didn't know how much longer she could keep it up. Then one day, she got an exciting phone call.

"I found your number on the Internet," the speaker said. "I'm looking for a cat actor." The voice belonged to a college student in Florida named Dana Buning. Dana was making a short movie for a class assignment. It was a scary movie called *Zeke* (sounds like ZEEK). It starred a man and his cat.

"Are you paying?" Samantha asked.

"Yes. We have a production budget," said Dana.

"We'll do it!" Samantha said with joy.

"Not so fast," Dana said. "Four other cats are trying out for the part. I need to see what Tuna can do."

Dana sent Samantha the script. Tuna was to play the bad guy. First off she had to look angry. That was easy. Tuna was naturally cranky. But she also needed to lick her mouth on cue. She had to snarl and pretend to bite. She had to lie flat on her back with her front legs stretched over her head. She needed to stay that way while other actors performed around her.

Samantha didn't know if Tuna would be okay sitting still for a big, scary camera on wheels. This role needed a brave cat.

Samantha decided that they would go for it. She taught Tuna to do everything the film needed. Tuna caught on fast.

Soon it was time to show the world Tuna's new tricks. Samantha had her perform for free to get her used to acting in strange places. The more shows Tuna did, the braver she got. Samantha recorded the shows and sent the videos to Florida. Dana studied them carefully. One day she called Samantha.

Yippee! Tuna got the part!

"The other cats are too nice," Dana said. "We like Tuna because she looks evil."

Two trips to Florida followed. Tuna worked hard. When the movie was done, she appeared in almost every scene.

Samantha was proud of her cat. She expected to hear from Hollywood any day.

But months passed and the phone didn't ring. "Don't worry, Tuna," Samantha said. "You'll get your chance. Just wait and see."

Tuna just blinked.

Samantha started taking the cat to a monthly film festival. She handed out flyers and set up a folding table to showcase Tuna. Sometimes show business people attended these movies. Maybe one of them would need a cat actor and Tuna would land another movie role.

In the meantime, Samantha taught Tuna to pluck a tiny guitar. One night, Samantha took the cat to a dinner theater. Dishes were clattering. People were talking. A hired band was playing in the next room. Samantha wondered if Tuna would perform.

But when she opened Tuna's carrier, hooray! The furry musician ran straight to her guitar. Tuna played like she was the only performer in the place.

Samantha had an idea. *I'll form an all-cat band,* she decided. She already had tiny instruments left over from her goose, duck, and chicken act. All she had to do was train some more cats to play them.

Did You Know?

In ancient Egypt, cats were made into mummies after they died.

The trouble was that Samantha's new cats were not like Tuna. Dakota, Pinky, and Nue jammed it up big time at home. But take them out in public? The scaredy-cats hid in their carriers.

Samantha wondered why the cats were so afraid. What could she do to make them feel safe? She tried offering different treats. That didn't work. Maybe she should ditch the band and form a duo with Tuna and just one other cat. That didn't work either.

Somehow Samantha had to make different performance spaces feel the same. Finally, she had an idea. She bought a sheet of soft vinyl (sounds like VINE-el) floor covering. At home she laid it out on her kitchen table and set up the band instruments on top. The cats got used to feeling the soft plastic under their feet.

When Samantha did a show, she rolled up the floor and took it with her.

Now the floor felt the same wherever they went. "They step on that," Samantha said, "and everything is okay."

One night she placed an ad on the Internet. "I have a Cat Circus act," she typed. "We need a place to perform."

A few days later, Samantha turned on her computer and bingo! A local art gallery was offering her space. She brought the roll of vinyl flooring and a cloth backdrop. The cats felt at home and played like rock stars.

People loved them. Soon other places invited them to perform.

Homeless No More

Animal shelters are full of unwanted cats and kittens. They can't hold any more. So many cats are put to death. This upsets Samantha. She saves lives by bringing kittens home and teaching them tricks.

Then she shows them off on stage. People clap and cheer. Some people ask to adopt the cats.

Samantha has found forever homes for 85 kittens. One of them is really special. She plays piano. "Whenever her owners come home," Samantha says, "she plays them a song!"

Samantha named her band The Rock Cats. They were the only all-cat band in America. The four meowers began playing several shows a week. Samantha crossed her fingers. She still believed that they could make it big if the right people noticed them.

One night a dog trainer called. He was somebody she had met two years earlier at the pet fair.

"A theater in Branson, Missouri, had an animal show booked," he said. "But the act backed out. I suggested they hire you to fill in."

"Branson! Wow!" Samantha pumped her fist in the air. She jumped up and down.

"Yahoo! Wake up, Tuna," she yelled. "This could be it—our big break!"

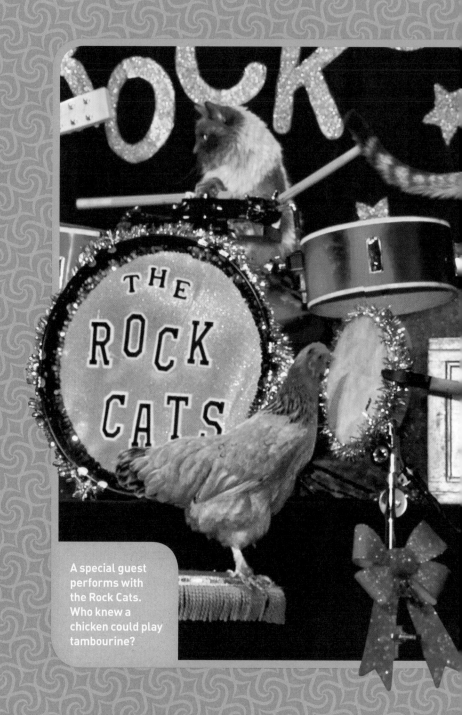

A special guest performs with the Rock Cats. Who knew a chicken could play tambourine?

Samantha and her assistant loaded heavy props into her old van. The last items they packed were pet carriers. These held 13 cats, a chicken, and a groundhog. Samantha had created an hour-long show. It included the Rock Cats band and a circus act called the Acro-Cats.

Just outside Branson, Samantha saw a billboard for a top-hatted man with many cats. It was world-famous Popovich (sounds like POP-OH-VITCH).

Come show time, hundreds of people poured into the theater. Workers passed out programs saying that the Rock Cats were replacing Popovich's Cat Circus. The audience was not happy. They had come to see Popovich.

Samantha felt nervous as she peeked out from behind the curtain. It was very tense backstage. There were two other animal acts. One of the trainers complained that Samantha's cats were after his birds. The other one hated Samantha's jumble of props.

Even Samantha's cats felt nervous.

The curtain went up. Samantha carried Tuna out on stage. Uh-oh! The furry superstar forgot her part. Tuna was supposed to open the show by pushing a lever that turned on a light. Instead, she chewed a foil bow stuck on a prop. "Your light, Tuna," Samantha urged. "Go to your light."

Tuna strolled over and lazily touched the lever. Nothing happened. Tuna started back toward her carrier.

The audience shifted in their seats.

"Tuna," Samantha said and motioned with her finger.

Tuna came halfway. She stretched and groomed herself.

"TUNA!" Samantha's face burned. Finally Tuna did what she was told. The light shone.

But it got worse. During their number, Dakota suddenly stopped drumming. "Phssssssst!" Her snarling bandmate swatted her.

It was a cat fight! On stage. In front of the crowd.

Tuna lifted her head, but she didn't join in. She quit ringing her bell. She used her paw to wash her face.

Samantha covered her eyes. "It's awful," she moaned. "Our show stinks."

The man who booked the Rock Cats took Samantha aside. "Get a costume," he told her. "Learn to go with the flow. When the cats go crazy, crack a joke."

Samantha nodded. But inside she worried. *Maybe I should get a normal job,* she thought.

Finally, this job was over. Samantha loaded up the van.

While Samantha drove home to Chicago, Tuna sat beside her with her back turned. Samantha knew better than to pet the cat. But she liked her company. She remembered Tuna's "killer stare" in the movie *Zeke*. She pictured the kitty ringing her bell on stage. And she thought about her long list of tricks.

Tuna is very smart, Samantha reminded herself. *She loves to perform. And she may be the best cat actress in America.*

Samantha smiled and straightened her back. She would keep trying.

For the next five years Samantha and her cats hit the road. They played art galleries and small theaters. With every show, Samantha got better with the audience.

Tuna didn't need to improve. She was already great.

Now it was spring 2012. The Acro-Cats were booked in a 500-seat theater in Santa Fe, New Mexico! That was almost as big as the theater in Branson. Samantha was so excited.

But Thursday night most of the seats were empty.

Even so, Tuna's performance was terrific. She ruled the stage!

Word spread. The crowd got bigger on Friday and Saturday. Then came Sunday.

Good Luck Cat

In Japan, people put a statue of a cat in their front window. It is called Maneki Neko (sounds like MA-NECK-EE NECK-O). It looks like a sitting cat waving goodbye. Except in Japan that kind of wave means, "Come here."

The statue reminds people of a pet cat said to have saved a man's life. People love that old story. And they use Maneki Neko as a good luck charm. Does it work? Probably not. But it honors cats, which is lucky for them.

A line of people stretched down the block. Grandmothers with walkers. Long-haired men in tie-dyed T-shirts. Girls in flip-flops. And young couples pushing strollers. Fifteen minutes before show time, the theater sold out.

Inside, the stage looked like a cat playground. Circus stools, tightropes, hurdles, ramps, and a crawl-through tube stood ready. Tiny instruments sat in front of a red curtain sprinkled with stars.

Lively music played. Samantha walked onstage. She wore a black cat suit and felt cat ears. "Here's Tuna!" she announced.

The furry superstar trotted out wearing a sparkly collar. She turned on her light. She stood on her hind legs and flipped open a welcome sign. Other cats entered.

They walked the high wire, rode skateboards, and climbed ropes.

The delighted crowd "oohed" and "aahed."

Now came the grand finale—the Rock Cats. "We have Pinky on guitar," Samantha said. "Dakota is on drums, and it's Nue on keyboard." She pointed to Tuna sitting down front with her upraised paw. "Tuna plays cowbell."

Samantha waved a stick and the "concert" began. These cool cats could not read music. And the sound they made? Better cover your ears. "They are a little tone deaf," said Samantha, smiling. "But they do all play together."

No sooner did Samantha speak than Dakota stopped playing. She ducked behind her drum. She looked like she was about to run off the stage.

Samantha knew what to do. She turned to the audience and grinned. "Cats want to be paid," she said. Then she handed Dakota a piece of chicken.

Dakota started the beat again and the audience cheered.

Then Tuna took over once more. She rang her bell and tapped her tip jar.

The crowd laughed out loud. Dozens of fans came to the stage and dropped in tips.

Tuna and the Rock Cats had finally done it. They had made the big time.

EEEE-YOW!

THE END

INDEX

MORE INFORMATION

To find more information about the animal species featured in this book, check out these books and websites:

Cats vs. Dogs, National Geographic, 2011

National Geographic Kids Everything Dogs, National Geographic, 2012

National Geographic "Animals: Domestic Cat" animals.nationalgeographic.com/animals/mammals/domestic-cat

National Geographic "Animals: Domestic Dog" animals.nationalgeographic.com/animals/mammals/domestic-dog

National Geographic "Animals: Groundhog" animals.nationalgeographic.com/animals/mammals/groundhog

Dunkirk Dave website and videos www.dunkirkdave.com

Rock Cats and Acro-Cats website and videos www.circuscats.com

This book is dedicated to my grandchildren,
Hannah and Chase,
who will always be superstars in my eyes.

CREDITS

ACKNOWLEDGMENTS

A special thank you to:

My ever-helpful husband, Neil, for taking such great groundhog pictures

Bob Will and Bill Verge, devoted groundhog rescuers

Samantha Martin, owner and manager of The Rock Cats

Michael Schelin, best friend of Opee, the Motocross Pup

Hope Irvin Marston, Judy Ann Grant, and Jule Lattimer, the members of my writers' group

Becky Baines, project editor, National Geographic Children's Books

About the author: www.alinealexandernewman.com

DON'T MISS!

**Turn the page
for a sneak preview . . .**

Binti Jua cradles her adorable baby, Koola.

Chapter 1

BOY MEETS GORILLA

It happened quickly, in less than half an hour. But for the parents of one little boy, those minutes felt like forever.

It was August 16, 1996. The mother and father had taken their son to the Brookfield Zoo near Chicago, Illinois. He was three years old. In the afternoon, the family went to see the gorillas. Seven gorillas were in the exhibit that day.

Binti Jua (sounds like BEN-tee WAH) was one of the females. She had a baby named Koola. Koola was 17 months old.

Have you ever seen a gorilla mother and baby together? They are so much fun to watch. Babies tug and tumble. They climb on their moms like jungle gyms. Then, quick as a wink, they cuddle and smooch. Gorilla mothers hug and kiss their babies. The babies hug right back. When they aren't playing or cuddling, gorilla babies ride on their mom's back.

Koola was so cute, she always drew big crowds. Everyone loved to visit her, especially kids. It was exciting.

That afternoon, the three-year-old boy got a little too excited. At one point, his mother looked away. It was only for a moment, but that was all it took. The small boy in a bright red shirt scrambled over the railing. Then, *THUNK*. He fell 18 feet (5.5 m)—almost two stories—down into the gorilla enclosure (sounds like in-KLOH-zhur). When he hit the concrete floor, he was knocked out. He lay there limp as a rag doll.

People gasped in horror. Everyone watching was afraid. No one knew what would happen next. No one knew just how to help. Someone ran to tell the zookeepers what had happened.

The little boy was in terrible danger. Gorillas may be fun to watch, but they are big and they are strong. They don't like surprises like tumbling little boys. Surprises sometimes make gorillas cranky.

Playtime

A newborn gorilla clings to its mother's chest for the first few months of life. Later, it learns to ride on her back. When gorillas turn three, they're ready for fun! Between the ages of three and six, gorillas act a lot like human children do. They spend most of their time playing. They climb trees and swing from branches. They wrestle and tumble. They chase each other round and round and scream with laughter. Sound like anyone you know?

People screamed in fear when one of the gorillas slowly walked toward the child. It was Binti Jua. Little Koola clung to her back.

A paramedic (sounds like pare-uh-MED-ik) named Bill Lambert was watching the gorillas, too. He was there when the boy fell. He even had his video camera rolling. Bill wanted to help the boy. He'd been trained to help in emergencies. But he couldn't reach the child. So he kept filming. He didn't know what to expect. What he captured was an amazing surprise.

It soon became clear that Binti Jua, called Binti for short, didn't want to hurt the boy. She wanted to help him.

Binti scooped up the child's small, still body in her big, furry arms. She carried him across a stream in the gorilla pen. Then she lifted him over a giant log. Binti headed to the zookeeper door at the back of the pen. When she got there, she cradled the boy in her right arm. Koola peeked at the boy from her spot on her mother's back. It was the tiny gorilla's turn to be curious.

The other gorillas also were curious about the boy. One of them growled at him. But Binti Jua wouldn't let the others get close to the child. She rocked him gently. She waited for help to arrive.

Craig Demitros was one of the gorilla experts at the zoo. He was eating lunch when his walkie-talkie went off. Signal 13—an emergency in the gorilla enclosure!

No one had ever fallen in there before, so Craig was surprised. But he knew what to do. He ordered three zookeepers to drive the gorillas into their rooms behind the pen. The zookeepers sprayed streams of water toward the gorillas. This didn't hurt them, but it did help them know which way to go. It also kept them away from Binti Jua and the boy.

Once the other gorillas left the pen, Binti Jua put the boy down. She was very careful with him. Then she followed the other gorillas into the back rooms. Koola still rode on her back.

Now the paramedics could do their job. They rushed the boy to the hospital.

Start to finish, the rescue took only 19 minutes. How did it go so well? The answer is practice, according to Craig. "Our team has safety walks through the enclosures to prepare for emergencies," he says. They'd practiced just a few days before the boy fell.

Being knocked out, or unconscious (sounds like un-CON-shus), also helped the boy. "Because he wasn't crying or screaming, he didn't seem to pose a threat," Craig says. "He also landed on his bottom, not his head. That may have saved his life."

Besides hurting his head, the little boy also had a broken hand. He spent three days in the hospital. Then the doctors said he was well enough to go home. But his parents never revealed his name. They did not want anyone to know who their son was.

For Binti Jua, it was the opposite. People everywhere learned her name. She became a star! Her heroic deed made headlines around the world. TV and radio programs around the world also featured her story.

The Brookfield Zoo's mailbox soon overflowed with letters about Binti Jua. "Congratulations with all our hearts," one group of kids wrote. Lots of kids wrote wanting to know more about her.

Binti even got fancy gifts. One gift was a sparkly, heart-shaped necklace. "Mother of the Year," it said.

Binti Jua munches on one of her favorite snacks. Do you think she knows she's famous?

Chapter 2

BRINGING UP BINTI

Everyone agrees that Binti Jua is a hero. But people still wonder why she did what she did. Why did she help the little boy? Curiosity is one theory (sounds like THEER-ee). Craig at the Brookfield Zoo says, "We think she was closest to where the boy actually fell in." So maybe Binti just wanted to check things out.

Or maybe she wanted to trade the boy—for a snack! Sometimes people drop things into the gorilla cage, like cameras and sunglasses. *Oops!* If the gorillas eat these things, it can make them very sick. So the zookeepers have trained the gorillas to bring things that fall into their cage to the zookeeper's door. As a reward, the apes get a yummy food treat. Maybe that's what Binti was hoping for. Maybe that's why she took the child to the door.

Craig says there could be another reason Binti was so gentle with the boy. It may have to do with the way she grew up.

Binti Jua was born in 1988 at the Columbus Zoo in Ohio. Her mother was a gorilla named Lulu. Her father's name was Sunshine. Binti was named after her father.

In the African language called Swahili (sounds like swah-HEE-lee), Binti Jua means "Daughter of Sunshine."

Lulu couldn't make enough milk to feed Binti. The zookeepers were afraid the baby wouldn't survive. So when Binti was three months old, they sent her to the San Francisco Zoo in California. Now she would be raised by humans.

For the rest of her first year, Binti lived with people, not gorillas. Human caretakers held her. Humans fed her. They played with her. They even slept with her. They were with her 24/7, just like a gorilla mother would be. According to the experts at the San Francisco Zoo, Binti Jua grew up feeling safe with humans. Maybe that's why she wasn't scared of the little boy.

As a baby, Binti even played with a little girl. The girl's name was Jennifer. Her mother worked at the zoo. When the two "kids" met, they reached their hands out to touch each other. It was like they were both human children. It was like they were both gorilla babies, too.

After her first birthday, Binti joined the rest of the gorillas at the San Francisco Zoo. It should have been a good thing. But Binti was sad and lonely. She was younger than the others. She didn't really know how to act around them. She bit a little too hard when she played. And she didn't stop playing when the grown-up gorillas got mad. She just didn't fit in. So the zookeepers decided to find her a new home.

Family Fame

Binti Jua isn't the only famous gorilla in her family. Her Aunt Koko is also a star. Koko lives at the Gorilla Foundation in Woodside, California. Her brother is Binti's father, Sunshine. What makes Koko the gorilla famous? She knows how to communicate using American Sign Language. Scientist Penny Patterson taught her how. Penny showed Koko the video of Binti saving the little boy. Then Penny asked her about Binti. Koko signed "lip"—that's her word for *girl*—and "good." In other words, Koko said Binti was a "good girl"!

When she was three years old, Binti moved to the Brookfield Zoo in Illinois. Everyone hoped it would be a better place for her.

Two other three-year-old gorillas lived at the Brookfield Zoo. The zookeepers hoped they would teach Binti Jua how to behave. It wasn't easy. "It was a school of hard knocks," Craig says. He means that Binti had to learn the hard way. She would scream and run. The other two little gorillas would slap and bite. Scream! Run! Slap! Bite! Binti took her lumps. Finally, she figured out how to act around the others. She learned good gorilla manners. Once she did, Binti was truly at home.

When Binti was six, zookeepers learned that she was expecting her first baby. They were excited. They were also a little worried. Binti had learned how to get along with other gorillas. But would she know how to be a gorilla mom? The zookeepers weren't sure.

Newborn gorillas are helpless and tiny. They weigh only about four pounds (2 kg) at birth. They need a lot of care from their mothers. Gorillas learn how to be mothers from their own mothers. But Binti wasn't raised by her mother, Lulu. She was raised by people. So she had to go to gorilla mommy school.

> **Want to know what happens next?**
> **Be sure to check out the**
> ***To the Rescue! Collection***

CREDITS

Title page, Lindsay Dancy-LDancy Design and Co-founder of Lilly Fund Boston, MA; BILL SUMNER; courtesy of Carolina Tiger Rescue; 3, Jim Schulz/Chicago Zoological Society; 7, Petra Wegner/Alamy; 13, Jim Schulz/Chicago Zoological Society; 18, Ron Cohn/Gorilla Foundation/koko.org; 21, Jim Schulz/Chicago Zoological Society